THROUGH THE DUST

Breaking
Leadership
Stereotypes

Idar & Jan   4-18-99

Rejoicing with you in
your victory over the
enemy & his distractions!
Thank you for serving
the couples in this class
of Married For Life!

Todd & Carol
Baker

THROUGH THE DUST

Breaking
Leadership
Stereotypes

Denny
Gunderson

YWAM Publishing
A Ministry of Youth With A Mission
P.O. Box 55787, Seattle, WA 98155

Dedication

To my late father, Carl Gunderson, and my mother, Wilma—loving partners together in over five decades of ministry.

With deep gratitude to....

Loren Cunningham, Floyd McClung, Jr., and Leland Paris—my three leaders in Youth With A Mission, all of whom exhibit true servant leadership.

Mr. Tom Marshall from New Zealand, whose wonderful lectures on leadership gave many fresh insights.

Geoff and Janet Benge, for their helpful advice, inspiration, and encouragement.

Dodie, Tanya, and Timmy, my wonderful family who showed exceeding patience during this project.

Table of Contents

Foreword

Denny Gunderson has managed to do two seemingly impossible things at the same time. He has written an unnervingly simply, yet deeply profound book that goes beyond your normal how-to leadership book.

This is no manual offering pious platitudes to make your church grow, nor is it a book written to make those of us who struggle with the complexities of leadership have a superficial, feel-good experience.

The values of the Kingdom of God, as fleshed out in the life of Jesus and other biblical biographies, call for a radical response. Denny does not preach at us, he simply tells the stories of Jesus and other biblical figures and applies the lessons contained therein to modern-day leadership paradoxes. His incisive insights cut across leadership dilemmas with profoundly simple, yet life-changing lessons.

Denny goes beyond answering the three classical leadership pitfalls—gold, gals, and glory—and gets to the deeper issues of a life-value system. Though every leader is susceptible to the above-mentioned temptations, a spiritual leader who has not allowed himself to be confronted with the Jesus of the New Testament and His Kingdom's value system will surely fail. Or to put it in Denny's words, "The temptation to gain special favor or to extend partial treatment can only weave its seductive spell upon the soul impressed with status."

Denny Gunderson draws upon a wealth of insight through his wide exposure to authors from many parts of the Body of Christ. The reader will be challenged to avail himself of many in the Body of Christ who are dissatisfied with power—models of leadership offered to us in our nation.

He probes the question of personal insecurity being mixed with ministry status and concludes that it is a combustible combination.

This book is a mirror, and in it we can see our own soul. I commend it to every leader who does not want more answers, but wants to be asking the right questions. I commend Denny Gunderson and the book he has written in a world filled with sham answers and superficial stereotypes. Both Denny and his book are for real.

Floyd McClung, Jr.
April 20, 1992

Through the Dust

The dust, driven through the air by powerful currents of wind, became tiny projectiles of destruction as they exploded upon the now helpless caravan. What had started as a promising trip to an adjoining city to trade cloth for pottery had abruptly become a living hell. The wail of fear emanating from the master's wife spoke for them all. They were helpless in the face of the storm's fury.

"Jehaziel! Jehaziel!" The master attempted to shout over the bellow of the wind. He hated to do it but knew that the minuscule hope remaining would soon be snuffed out unless his servant Jehaziel attended to duty.

By now, the heaving volumes of dust had blocked out the light of the sun, and it was almost impossible to breathe. A kind of vertigo was setting in. Man and beast alike were becoming disoriented. All sense of direction was lost.

Many in the caravan were gasping with the exertion of maintaining order among the animals. The beasts were close to panic. If not restrained, they would make a mad dash for shelter and would perish in the desert. Maybe in the distant future, Bedouins would stumble across their decomposed bodies.

"Master! Hang on. I'm here." The words were squeezed from between cracked lips, barely audible. But loud enough to arouse the master from his gruesome reverie.

"Jehaziel? My wife's on behind me. It's up to you. You know I'll reward you handsomely." The sound of the master's voice was cruelly cut off by the wind's omnipotent force. All he could do was hold on for dear life, hoping his wife could, too. Their survival now rested solely in the hands of their servant.

It was days later...or was it only hours? The camel groaned, then struggled to its feet. Its burden slid unimpeded to the ground. "Ahhh." The involuntary cry caused the beast's ears to prick up. Slowly, the heap of tangled clothing began to move, then separated as husband and wife rose unsteadily, groping for each other. Tragedy had struck, but at least they were still alive.

Slowly and painfully their swollen eyes attempted to focus. The effort drew tears down their faces as vision strained to return. They seemed to be partially shielded to the east by an outcropping of rock.

"We made it!" croaked the man, looking at his wife. Then he noticed the anguish in her eyes as she stared over his shoulder. Turning, he followed his wife's line of sight.

"Oh, no!" he cried. Lying half-buried in the sand was the familiar figure of their loyal servant Jehaziel, his body frozen in the stiff posture of death.

They fell to their knees in silent memorial. It was now apparent that their beloved servant Jehaziel had unflinchingly confronted the terrifying sandstorm, in the process giving up his own life that they might live. He had served them once again, this time by leading the way through the dust in order to find shelter for his master.

It is from this scenario that the Greek word for servant, *diakonos*, comes. *Diakonos* consists of two words. *Dia* means "through or across," just as diameter is a measurement through the center of a circle. *Konos* may be translated as "dust, dirt, or earth." Thus, *diakonos* literally means "through the dust." Diakonos is the word Jesus used as He responded to James and John as they sought preferment in the new Kingdom: "If anyone wants to be first, he must be the very last, and the servant of all" (Mark 9:35).

Remarkably enough, Jesus had little to say regarding leadership, and even less about how to attain it. His few references to leaders are primarily negative, leaving one with the impression that He viewed leadership as having secondary importance at best.

Whenever the disciples fell into dispute about leadership positions, Jesus refused to dignify their discussion with direct answers, preferring instead to demonstrate servanthood. It is little wonder that most contemporary Christian books on leadership shy away from using Jesus as the model for leadership, choosing rather to focus on Moses, David, Nehemiah, or Paul (the few exceptions will be noted in this book).

The relative silence of Jesus regarding leadership, however, should not be interpreted as meaning that leadership is a non-biblical concept. Indeed, the testimony of the whole of Scripture is that God has gifted and called people to lead. Those who believe that leadership is strictly a gift usually argue the point that leaders are "just born that way." In opposition to this, those who emphasize that leadership is a call argue that it is a skill to be learned.

Plenty of evidence can be marshaled on both sides of this argument. Therefore, it is quite possible that this point of antagonism is not really that important. What is of paramount importance is the quality of service rendered by those men and women having leadership roles, however they were acquired.

The subtitle to this book is "Breaking Leadership Stereotypes." There are many stereotypes today surrounding leadership in the Body of Christ. Some of the more common stereotypes are:

- Good leaders must embody the ability to "take charge."
- Good leaders should take advantage of every opportunity to promote their ministry.
- Good leaders should focus their attention on straightening other people out.
- Good leaders work hard to get to the top and are therefore deserving of special ministry privileges.
- Good leaders keep an appropriate distance between themselves and their followers.
- Good leaders must have preaching as their top priority.
- Good leaders should be good entrepreneurs.
- Good leaders see to it that followers do not challenge their position.
- Good leaders know that it takes years of preparation, study, and training before a person can be trusted with leadership responsibility.

This list is by no means exhaustive. What we shall find as we go along, however, is that *diakonos* cuts against the grain of our leadership stereotypes.

Jesus is unarguably the greatest Leader that the world has ever seen. His three years of public ministry in an obscure and troublesome corner of the Roman Empire not only irrevocably changed Roman civilization, but every other civilization that has subsequently emerged. And the only stereotype one can find for Jesus' leadership is *diakonos*.

Chapter One

Letting Go
(Matthew 3; John 3)

Azor could not deny the hint of expectancy that hung in the air—a restless waiting filled with nervous energy. He had felt it for many months, ever since he had joined with the Baptist. But now, more and more people clustered around the Baptist every day, listening intently, yet with the pervading sense that something lingered just beyond their grasp.

As Azor stooped to pick a stone out of his sandal, his eyes met those of a small boy whose mother supported him as he hopped along on one leg. The other leg was a swollen, lifeless mass. Azor smiled at them. Two sets of hopeful eyes radiated back at him. Azor understood their plight. Surely the Baptist would pray for the young one.

Azor stood and surveyed the crowd. About 500 people squeezed together on the river's muddy banks. For days now, people had been flocking here to see the Baptist. Azor thought back to the first time he had seen him. Something about the Baptist had awakened musty memories of patriarchal figures from a mythical past. It wasn't just his unconventional visage, stern and eccentric as it was. The people were used to such images, having for years observed the studied religiosity of Pharisees, Sadducees, and sundry other holy men.

Perhaps it had been John's eyes, at times flashing with excited ecstasy, but more often smoldering with the naked intensity of a person compelled by a long-awaited message. The message itself was so compellingly simple: the long awaited one, the Messiah, would be here soon, and John the Baptist was to herald His arrival.

Azor wondered often about this. Would he be one of Abraham's most blessed descendants who would truly see the awaited one? What would the Messiah be like? Surely He would be like the Baptist. And if the Baptist could gather such crowds on his own, how much bigger would they be with the Messiah beside him? What a glorious moment! And according to the Baptist, the hour was nearly upon them.

"He's coming," trilled the high-pitched voice of a mud-splattered street urchin. The clusters of people wheeled as one, becoming mob-like as they hurriedly vied for vantage points along the river bank. The cacophonous din of voices, tumbling words, yapping dogs, and running feet echoed across the valley.

The determined stride of the Baptist propelled him down the bank and into the stream. For a moment, he surveyed the rabble facing him. Then he exclaimed, "Repent, for the kingdom of God is near."

Some in the crowd were transfixed while others nudged their neighbors in the ribs, sharing knowing smiles of delight at the audacity of what they were hearing. Something in the air portended change, a possible shifting of the established order.

"...But he will burn up the chaff with unquenchable fire." The words reverberated with detached bluntness. The throng shifted self-consciously, the preacher's gaze holding their attention though his lips were now silent. Azor never tired of hearing the

Baptist. Each time he stood before the ever burgeon-
ing crowd, it was as if he were unfolding history, not
merely imparting words.

Momentarily, Azor became aware of a minor distraction taking place. Quickly he shouldered his way
through the crowd. The hair on the back of his neck
raised in warning. What would it be this time? Always
at the back of his mind were fears of retaliation by the
Pharisees. Surely they would not tolerate the scathing
remarks unendingly. Maybe it would just be the mad-
man bound with ropes who was dragged here daily
by his family. Often the Baptist said something which
disturbed him, and the man became uncontrollable,
throwing the weight of his body at those around him.

As Azor approached the center of the distraction,
he noticed several of John's other disciples making
their way there, too. He made a mental note of their
positions, relieved that there were enough of them to
deal with any situation.

Surprisingly, the distraction seemed to revolve
around a Man winding His way through the jostling
crowd. It wasn't the Man Himself who was making
the commotion. There was nothing unique about His
appearance and from a distance, He looked no different from dozens of similarly-aged men sprinkled
among the bystanders. He was of average build and
wore clothing befitting the common man. He walked
purposefully, oblivious to the reactions of those
around Him. Azor moved into step behind Him, puzzled as the crowd parted for the Man to pass.

When at last the Stranger came into the Baptist's
view, a look of recognition flashed between them.
"My cousin," breathed the Baptist.

The Stranger nodded. "It has been a long time. It
is fitting for you to baptize Me now, John."

A look of confusion passed across the Baptist's

face. In a split second of cosmic insight the face of his cousin was transformed from one of physical familiarity into a countenance that seemed sketched by some timeless artist with strokes from eternity.

"Jesus! You are the One." It was a statement made more for his own endorsement than anyone else's. The Baptist spoke in a tone which Azor had never heard him use; a tone of wonder tinged with a trace of shock.

The Stranger's eyes locked with the Baptist's. Azor felt uneasy. This was not the way others had approached baptism. The Sadducees tended to rip off their tunics and offer long, loud prayers, while many of the women wept and clung to the Baptist. As Azor watched, it struck him that this Stranger and the Baptist were playing out some preordained act, each honoring the other as they did so.

It wasn't until later that evening that the Baptist finally spoke to his disciples about the day's bewildering events. Everything had happened so quickly; the voice from the sky, the dove hovering over the Stranger's head, the uncharacteristic quiet that came over the normally boisterous crowd. It had been eerie, and as quickly as the Stranger had appeared, He disappeared again into the dusty landscape. Things seemed normal again, but in his heart Azor knew the events had somehow changed the Baptist forever.

Now for the first time, John was going to speak to them about it. But before he could, one of the group blurted out, "Was that Him, the One you have been telling us about?" No one had to articulate who the "Him" was, which reminded Azor that this Stranger had made an unparalleled impression.

"What was His name? People say you are related to Him? Is that true?"

The Baptist positioned himself on a rock. "Yes. His name is Jesus and He is my relative. My mother and

His mother are cousins. But I have not seen Him for many years, not since we were young boys."

"Does He know who you are?" asked Azor anxiously. "I mean, about your miraculous birth and the promise to your parents?" Azor, like many from the region, had heard the story of Elizabeth's conception late in life, and of his father's muteness, given as a reminder of his unbelief. Many times John's followers had bolstered each other's faith with a reminder of the Baptist's unique place in God's sight.

The Baptist nodded. "But I also know who He is."

"When is He going to begin His reign?" another anxious disciple asked.

"Do I have time to return to my village for my sword?"

"Do you think He wants to wipe out the Romans or merely make Jewish slaves of them?"

"Baptist, He will make you His first in command, won't He? Isn't that what He talked to you about?"

"Will we get extra privileges? After all, we have been in this from the beginning."

The questions flew rapidly at John. The disciples were in awe. History and destiny were now flowing as one, and they were in the center of it all.

The state of excitement escalated over the next few days. Jesus came back several times to speak with the Baptist, and each time the disciples waited for the inevitable summons. Some became anxious at the deliberate evasiveness of the Baptist. Either he did not know what was about to happen, or he was unwilling to share his knowledge with the group. Either option was very disconcerting.

Almost imperceptibly, a change began taking place. This shifting of focus culminated for Azor when he noticed Jesus preaching, not with John, but further down the river, in apparent opposition. Panicked, he ran back to the Baptist.

"That Man who was with you on the other side of the Jordan—Jesus. Well, He's preaching further down the river, and everyone is going to see and hear Him." The statement came tumbling out, a sign of Azor's growing frustration. The silent implication of his statement was both a challenge and a question: "What are you going to do about it?"

A bemused but patient look settled upon the Baptist's face. "A man can receive only what is given him from heaven." The tone of his voice held no rebuke, just simple instruction. "You yourselves can testify that I said, 'I am not the Christ, but am sent ahead of Him.' The bride belongs to the bridegroom."

The people within range of his voice strained closer, captivated by his words and the look of adoration shining on the Baptist's face.

"The friend who attends the bridegroom waits and listens for him, and is full of joy when he hears the bridegroom's voice. That joy is mine, and it is now complete!" His voice rang with triumph. Some in the small audience were transfixed, their mouths parted like baby birds waiting to be fed. Others lingered, not really understanding, but sensing they were in the presence of someone who knew.

Then John the Baptist averted his gaze and looked beyond the mortal realm. With a quiet but sure voice, he spoke to all mankind and said, "He must increase, but I must decrease."

The human obsession for control and the sincere desire of a true leader to serve are mutually exclusive.

Our story of John the Baptist began at a pivotal moment in human history. John was a man widely listened to and respected by the populace; he spoke with authority and certainty. Many even wondered if he was the awaited one.

Jews traveled great distances to hear John the Baptist, and many were being transformed by his teaching. Thus it was only natural that they should look to him to validate their observations of Jesus.

When John met Jesus, he had a choice to make: he either had to direct people to Jesus, with the eventual result of smothering his own ministry, or he could retain control of the situation by discrediting Jesus. In choosing to acknowledge Jesus as the One for whom he had been waiting, and in encouraging people to follow Jesus, John initiated the demise of his own ministry.

Nothing is more disheartening to the soul than to be at the pinnacle of seeming greatness, the expectancy of grandeur dancing delightedly in one's mind, only to be dashed unexpectedly by the realization that you are no longer needed. I believe it is safe to speculate that this is what John the Baptist experienced. The thrill of knowing that at last the Messiah had arrived, and with Him the fulfillment of long-awaited prophecies, was rudely interrupted for John by the reality of dwindling crowds.

While we are not able to herald Christ to the world in the same way John was, we are each called to make the same choice as he. As leaders, we are called to decrease on two levels.

The first level is choosing Jesus' way of doing things over "our" ministry and the way we like to do things. The second is choosing to let someone else take a task or position we presently hold, and not being threatened when they do a better job.

The question is, will we make the right choice? Are we willing to decrease in order that the other person might increase, or does our ego stand in the way? God often requires a diminishing of our role just as we feel we are at last about to achieve our destiny. But He requires it always with our highest good in mind and in spite of our bitter protestations.

This fact was brought home to me with startling clarity several years ago. A ministry which I had started began to lose momentum. I recall the distinct agony of literally watching the disintegration of the ministry I felt I had given birth to. Funds began to dry up. The enrollment at our training schools began to drop. Staff morale began to decline.

At first, I responded normally by endeavoring to rally the troops and assure everyone that we were just under the Enemy's attack. Eventually, however, the realization began to dawn upon me that regardless of other mitigating factors, God was attempting to wean me from the obsessive need to be in charge. He wanted to realign my thoughts and actions. He wanted me to see that any success I may have been enjoying was because He was in control, and not because I had achieved it through my own efforts. Despite this, a voice in the back of my mind kept bombarding me with the unwelcome idea that if the ministry failed, my reputation and standing as a leader would be irreparably damaged.

But God was more interested in developing my character and my reliance upon Him than in giving me a ministry or position that enhanced feelings of prestige. Consequently, a few of the remaining leaders and I decided it was time to allow the ministry to die—totally! We actually closed things down and suggested that our staff seek guidance from the Lord as to where they should go. This was not a case of abdicating our responsibility or of seeking to cover up our failure. Rather, it was an honest attempt to face the uncomfortable reality that decay had come into a once-thriving ministry. As the primary leader, I had to embrace failure and come to grips with a side of myself that I did not want to see.

M. Scott Peck points out that, "The need for control—to ensure the desired outcome—is at least partially rooted in the fear of failure."[1] Now, with the understanding only retrospect can bring, I clearly see that God was attempting to deal with the fear of failure in my life.

I had been a leader for years. Yet in spite of growing competence and ability, I was too insecure to face this fear. Deep within my soul was a desperate desire to prove that I deserved to be a leader, and the idea of failing as a leader was absolutely abhorrent. The result was bondage to performance-oriented ministry, and it had become a cruel and exacting taskmaster.

Over the years I have had to participate as a troubleshooter in a number of scenarios similar to my own. In those rare instances when a leader could not face his failure or weakness, the damage always had a long-term affect.

"John" started a church in the name of an evangelical movement. Soon, though, John began to stray from the organization's basic values and stated on numerous occasions that he, a relative newcomer, wanted to change the way the denomination did things.

There is no problem in wanting to implement positive change in methodology and technique. But for a newcomer to desire to reinvent the very foundation stones of a ministry is an entirely different matter.

As an objective outsider from another organization, I was asked to help bring mediation. I watched as John's leaders lovingly confronted him about the situation. They received many promises, but nothing changed. John seemed to have too much of his ego and personal agenda tied up in the situation to willingly relinquish any of his "rights."

Very painfully, things went from bad to worse, until a final "showdown" was inevitable. At the showdown, John handed in his resignation.

It would have been wonderful to imagine the problem was solved with John's resignation, but it had only just begun. John did anything he could to sabotage the ministry. He had many wonderful qualities which could have been a real asset to his ministry, but he could not step out and trust God in the area of relinquishing control. And if he wasn't going to be in control of the ministry, then he was determined that no one else would be, either. In other words, he was only willing to see the ministry prosper if it would be run his way.

As I reflected upon this dilemma, I realized that Solomon had faced a similar problem (see I Kings 3:16-28). Two women and a baby were brought before Solomon, each woman claiming to be the baby's mother. To end the dispute "fairly," Solomon ordered a sword with which to cut the baby in half. One of the women objected, asking that the baby's life be spared and that the child be given to the other woman. Solomon knew that the one who had spoken must be the real mother. Why? Because she loved the child enough to choose his welfare over her own.

This biblical account contains real parallels to the situation we faced with John. When confronted with the thought that the ministry would go on without his leadership, John did everything within his power to see it "killed." It was an extreme situation, but fortunately the ministry survived as new leadership took on the challenge of resuscitation.

It is easy for us to judge John for his actions, but if we are honest and look closely at ourselves, we may find similar seeds within each of our hearts. How will we react when faced with the choice of losing our importance, status, position, or prominence in order to preserve a ministry or allow someone else's input into it? Would we make that choice or would we cling on to the bitter end, milking the prestige of our position for every last drop of prideful self-fulfillment until we are finally forced out?

There are times when God calls us to decrease in order to elevate others. Making this choice requires an implicit trust in God's faithfulness. We must acknowledge that He is the One who ultimately controls our destinies. If we truly believe that God is at the helm of our destiny, then we can easily lay aside our ego struggles and the organizational politics that can so insidiously creep into the Christian leader's life.

One of the deepest fears in the human psyche, particularly for leaders, is the fear of not being in control. Such a fear stands in stark contrast to one of the basic principles of servant leadership: The servant leader is one who chooses to decrease by willingly laying aside his own ego in order to champion the ministry of others.

I am not suggesting that to be a servant leader we should arbitrarily and repeatedly abdicate our God-given role of leadership. I am suggesting, however, that there should be a constant willingness to step aside should God indicate the wisdom in doing so. This may require the relinquishment of a prized position, leaving the security of a solid financial "power base," or voluntarily minimizing our own importance so that someone else can have opportunity to rise to a place of prominence.

The true servant, with nothing to prove and no vested interest, takes joy in seeing others grow beyond himself. In the words of Henri Nouwen, "The beginning and the end of all Christian leadership is to give your life for others."[2]

The sovereignty of God makes no allowance for accidents. It surely is not incidental that the onset of Jesus' public ministry was heralded by one whose own ministry began to quietly recede into the gray background of relative unimportance. That is where theory and reality kiss. The syrupy appeals to "die to self" spoken across the land on Sunday mornings move into harsh reality on Monday morning with that unexpected loss of self-importance.

Could it be that God is actually looking for leaders who are willing to lead by knowing when to take a back seat? Is it possible that a living demonstration of selflessness could make a greater contribution to promoting New Testament leadership values than our eloquent verbiage and natural gift for decisive action?

A commitment to planned obsolescence may produce inferior automobiles, but it makes for great servant leaders. Of course, true servants by their very nature can never be truly obsolete. In reality, the growth of godly influence spreads exponentially in proportion to our willingness to not be recognized and rewarded. Are we willing to walk this narrow path, knowing that it could mean the relinquishment of our dreams of fame, glory, and fulfillment?

God, in sovereign wisdom, allows spiritual leaders to be tested repeatedly on the point of leadership identity. Simply stated, the test is this: Are we willing to embrace God's will, even when His will appears to hold a deterioration of our personal place of importance as a leader? Is our identity so wrapped up in our leadership position that the loss of that position causes deep emotional trauma?

John the Baptist must have gone through this test. He watched most of his disciples and followers "de-fect" to Jesus, and then within a short time he went on to his own imprisonment and death. Yet John stayed true to the statement he had made, "He must increase, I must decrease." It's rather like being on a seesaw: only one person can be up in the air at a time. If we promote ourselves, even unwittingly, we automatically demote Jesus. There are times when we must make the same choice John made.

Chapter Two

Walking Away
(Mark 1)

When battling insomnia, Simon usually would have gone to the back of the house and climbed the stairs to the roof. He had spent many nights up there, staring out over the city. Capernaum was never completely quiet, often mimicking his own restless spirit. But tonight was different.

There was no way he could mount the stairs. If he were to step outside his mother-in-law's door he would be barraged by more questions. It was impossible to say from looking out the west window, but he guessed there must be at least 300 people sprawled out across the street. Some were sitting on bed rolls. The temple beggars were there. A small child began to cry and was quickly silenced by his mother's breast. Many of the neighborhood men were crouched in small groups, talking in excited tones.

Simon knew exactly how they felt. Although he had been traveling with the Master for several weeks now, nothing had prepared him for this day. It was too mind boggling, too overwhelming to take in. He thought back to how he had come to be involved with the Master.

He and the three others had felt a glowing sense of calm about the Master. And when He said to them,

"Follow Me and I will make you fishers of men," to Simon it had seemed the only right thing to do. None of them knew exactly what a "fisher of men" was. It didn't really matter at the time.

But this...today....It went beyond anything Simon could have imagined. He thought back over the morning's events. The Master had stood in the synagogue to teach. He taught in the same way He had called them to follow Him: with authority and purpose. How different from the scribes who had the unique ability to say nothing in ten different ways!

With all the attention the Master attracted, nobody had noticed Galal, the maniac, slip in. Simon's mother-in-law had told Simon that it took several men to calm Galal down once he got started, and that the Pharisees had banned him from being in the synagogue at all.

Just when the Master was reaching the climactic point of His sermon, Galal had begun one of his screaming tirades. "Why are You here, Jesus of Nazareth? Have You come to destroy us all?" Simon had been standing near the Master, and he watched His reactions closely. Without fear or even irritation, the Master had looked over at Galal and with magisterial calm had said, "Be silent and come out of him!"

Galal's body had contorted, and he fell to the ground as if twisted by some great invisible hand. After a blood-chilling scream and some whimpering, Galal was silent.

Finally, Galal raised his head and looked around as if he had just awakened from a deep sleep. And then...he smiled peacefully. The Master had looked deeply into his eyes, acknowledging his smile before He continued reading from Isaiah's scroll.

Simon had scarcely heard another word as the Master read on. Just who was this Man they were following? What would He do next? And more to the point, what would He require of them if they stayed with Him? Simon's imagination had already been stretched so much that he wasn't sure he could absorb any more.

Simon had slipped out to ask his mother-in-law if the group of them could lodge at her house, only to find her very ill with a high fever. Her eyes were sunken and her clothes were soaked with perspiration. He had no idea how long she had lain there alone, but there was no more water in the jar, nor was there bread to eat.

Simon had run back and pushed through the crowd to reach the Master, who immediately followed him back to the house. The Master had gone in and greeted Simon's mother-in-law. As He had reached out and taken her hand in His, strength had seemed to flow through it to her, and she immediately stood up and offered to fetch water for them.

As the day turned into evening, the news of the Master's whereabouts spread rapidly. A stream of sick, diseased, and possessed people were brought to the door, and the street began to take on a carnival-like atmosphere.

That evening the power of God was displayed in ways that the inhabitants of Capernaum had never seen or heard. Indeed, even those who knew the ancient Scriptures well could not recall an instance when anything of this magnitude had happened in their forefathers' day. There were recorded healings of course, like Naaman's leprosy and Hezekiah's life being extended, but absolutely nothing of the scale they were now experiencing. After all, there was not a person in the entire city who did not have a relative or friend affected by this Rabbi.

And now, with the sun set behind the western hills,

it seemed the entire town of Capernaum had gathered around the house of Simon's mother-in-law. And that was part of Simon's dilemma.

No wonder he couldn't settle down. There was so much planning to be done. The Master seemed very vague when it came to handling crowds. It had almost gotten out of hand earlier in the evening. Surely, Simon reasoned, it would be best if he took on the role of organizer.

He thought how smart it was for the Master to choose Capernaum as the headquarters for His ministry. Set on the edge of the Sea of Galilee, it was the commercial and social center for the surrounding area. It was a perfect location and the Master had certainly made a deep impression on the city. His actions in the synagogue had shown His great power to the priests as well as the common people—there was no denying it.

Simon cradled his head in his hands as he mulled over the implications of the day's events. Sleep was far from him.

It was well before dawn when the Master arose from His bed. He tied His bedroll together and walked over to where Simon was sitting, glancing out the window as he did so.

"Hand Me your cloak, Simon, so the people don't recognize Me. I need to go and be alone with My Father."

Simon looked up, startled. "Certainly, Rabbi," he said, handing over his cloak.

The Master wrapped the large black garment tightly around Himself and raised the hood over His head. "When you have need of it, you may take Mine," He said to Simon, gesturing to the gray cloak by the door. Then He quietly unlatched the door and slipped unnoticed into the darkness.

Morning finally arrived. Even with a minimal amount of sleep, Simon felt energized by the need to organize this new and exciting day. Outside, the crowd was beginning to chant the Master's name, calling for Him to come out and minister to them.

Many of those with infirmities began to get agitated when the Master did not emerge from the house. Simon empathized with them. And where was the Master? There was so much for Him to do—demons to be cast out, people to be healed.

James and John inquired as to the Master's whereabouts. "You mean you let the Rabbi go out alone?" James chastised Simon when he heard that the Master had left well before dawn.

"How was I to know He wouldn't be back by now?" Simon countered. "What did you expect me to do? Hold Him here?"

John, seeing the rise of explosive tempers, offered a solution. "Well, we could go and get Him now. Perhaps He is already conducting a meeting down at the marketplace."

"I'll go," offered Simon. "I let the Master go off alone, so I will bring Him back."

It took longer than expected before Simon found the Master. In fact, if he hadn't recognized his own cloak, Simon probably would not have even stopped to see if the Man sitting alone under an olive tree was the Master. "Come on, we have to get back," Simon urged. His face was animated by a flush of relief and excitement. "Everyone is looking for You."

Instead of erupting into a frenzy of activity at the realization that He had stayed too long, the Master motioned for Simon to sit down.

"It is time for us to go on to the next town now, Simon. I must preach in many places, for that is the reason I came."

Simon was astounded. Every door of opportunity in Capernaum was open. Why not stay? There would be plenty of time to visit other cities later.

The Master rose and began walking in a southerly direction toward Gennesaret. Simon did not know whether to go back and get the others or stay with the Master. How could He do this? What more could He want? Simon grimaced as he realized his mother-in-law was expecting them any moment for a meal, and there were all manner of people waiting to talk with the Master and see Him perform miracles.

Simon vacillated for a moment and then begrudgingly fell into step behind the Rabbi. There was no use going back to the city. What would he say? How would he explain the Master's strange behavior? What was it that the Master really wanted? It had all fitted so perfectly into place yesterday, but now it was just the two of them trudging unrecognized through an olive grove.

Obedience and humility are God's twin guardians against the plague of vain ambition resident within the heart of the leader who wants to be a star.

The writer to the Hebrews says, "For we do not have a high priest who is unable to sympathize with our weaknesses, but we have one who has been tempted in every way, just as we are—yet was without sin" (Hebrews 4:15). How often we use this verse to help ward off the temptation toward the "external sins" of lying, cheating, adultery, and the like. But the verse says emphatically that Jesus was tempted by every temptation with which we are faced.

Imagine you were Jesus in Capernaum. What would you have done? You have just attracted an entire city by your ministry. You have performed mind-boggling miracles and stand at the center of all activity. What a wonderful way to go from unknown to big time in one step.

You or I might argue that God's anointing and blessing were obviously shining down on us, so it would only be appropriate to "seize the moment." But Jesus refused to submit to conventional wisdom. His disciples, however, had been dazzled by their Master's exploits and would have stopped at nothing to feed the machinery of publicity.

You or I would probably have done the same. As members of the Church in the western world, we have been seduced by the pragmatic efficiency of the world's system. This time the culprit is corporate leadership technique, American-style.

It is indeed difficult to argue with a system that works, delivering on its promise to produce results which satisfy the three pillars of success in America— size, speed, and public exposure. In our anxious desire to validate the "fruit" of our ministries, we have given in to this unholy trinity. We justify methods which in effect do a tragic disservice to God, the very One in whose Name we are ministering. Undoubtedly, there is not a person among us who has been spared the temptation of placing ego above obedience!

Doorways of opportunity can quickly become trap doors for the leader driven to promote his ministry. The enticement of success and popularity can easily delude a leader into believing the fallacy that opportunity and guidance are synonymous. Add to this the clamoring expectations of followers, and an almost irresistible pull develops which can easily lure a leader away from accomplishing the true will of God.

I am certain Jesus faced the temptation to "sell out" to fast results. Yet it seems He was almost oblivious to ministry momentum, not because of anything

He said, but by His refusal to capitalize on the situations and opportunities created.

Why was this? What force exerted itself in Jesus' life that pulled Him away from the temptation to sell out? By extension, we understand that this same force can save us from falling into the pit of materialism and showmanship as opposed to servant leadership. The answer is simple. One principle alone guided Jesus' response to any situation: "The one who sent me is with me; he has not left me alone, for I always do what pleases him" (John 8:29).

By putting the Father's will above His own, Jesus dwelt in that serene place where ego, prestige, and position had no dominion. James reminds us that a double-minded person is unstable in all his ways. But Jesus was no double-minded person. He was resolutely single-minded and had only one agenda: to fulfill the will of His Father.

Each of us must ask the Holy Spirit to search our hearts and reveal to us those things we are doing, often in His name, which are not in accordance with God's guidance for our lives. Constrained by love for Jesus, we must seek to order everything in accordance with His will, even if it means forfeiting wonderful opportunities to further enhance our leadership standing. We must have the courage and conviction to say "no" to a coveted opening, even when knowing that by doing so another leader may take our place in reaping the "rewards."

Why do we find it so difficult to emulate Jesus' leadership style in this regard? A cursory glance over the last five years of "Christian" headlines is enough to convince even the most rabid Evangelical that leaders often do put aside their pure calling in order to play the "Gain and Fame Game."

I believe there are a number of reasons why we so

frequently reject the Jesus-model of leadership.

First, the natural mind of western man is obsessed with formula and technique. Jesus' way of leading is so radically different that we cannot fit Him into a comfortable equation that fits our preconceptions as to what leadership looks like. Our very human desire to maintain our personal comfort zone drives us to concoct simplistic formulas by which to categorize life. Thus, we tend to categorize leadership in terms of charisma, boldness, or natural ability—none of which necessarily relate to servanthood.

Second, the very nature of servant leadership goes deeply against the grain of human ego. In our current sophistication (i.e., pride) we have mastered the abilities of cover-up and spiritualization to such a degree that we offer mere lip-service to the possibility of pride while denying its insidious work in our hearts.

It is simple to use the language of servanthood. Indeed, it is currently in vogue to do so. Phrases such as, "I just want to serve you," and "I just want to be a nobody for Jesus," are spoken with great piety countless times each day. Watch out for the nobodies! If one has to say it, he is probably not doing it! Hidden agendas are usually cloaked in enticing dialects. It is quite possible to attain a little self-glory by proper usage of evangelical vernacular, but there is absolutely no glamour in the hard work of service.

Third, our utter concentration upon "success" fuels us with a tainted incentive to look good. Working feverishly, we sacrifice the future in order to look good today. We make promises and announce big plans we cannot possibly bring about, but we sound and look successful. The problem is that servant leadership cannot fit into the straitjacket of immediate results, as its environment is the rarefied realm of the long range.

A close friend and I were once involved in a facetious dialogue about how easy it is to impress people. Our conclusion was that as long as you talk a lot about your grand schemes and visions, people will tend to view you as successful, in spite of the absence of fruit that remains. In America, appearance counts more than reality. We even have books that instruct us how to dress in order to look successful, the implication being that as long as you look like a winner, the actuality is superfluous.

Is it proper then for the potential leader to have a sense of destiny or ambition? The answer is a qualified "yes," if one understands destiny to mean God-given direction and vision.

One's destiny also becomes one's test, however. The person driven to act out and prove that he is God's specially called man (or woman) can easily forfeit his anointing to lead. The initial calling may well be from God, but when stained by human ego, destiny degenerates into the fetid stench of empire-building, and empire-builders have the unfortunate tendency of ending up as false prophets! In other words, vain ambition can so easily disguise itself as vision that the one propagating the vision may well be deceived by his own words.

The leader who wishes to emulate Jesus resists the great temptation to build a ministry around himself. He chooses to abandon himself to the will and pleasure of God on a moment by moment basis. Thus, communion takes precedence over causes, and obedience over opportunity. Leadership pleasing to God is reserved for those servants willing to enter the crucible of divine dictate, often forfeiting opportunities for advancement in the process.

For as long as he could remember, my dear friend Bob Ogle had wanted to be a missionary. He came to our mission center in Tacoma, Washington, and soon became a very valuable member of our leadership team. It wasn't long before God led Bob out to the Caribbean Basin, where Youth With A Mission was pioneering several new works. Again, Bob's qualities were quickly recognized and he became Director for the Caribbean region.

After several years, Bob felt that God was directing him to leave the mission and take care of some debts that had accumulated. Some of his fellow missionaries tried to dissuade him. He had a very responsible position. Didn't he know that our work in the Caribbean region was growing rapidly? If Bob left the mission, he would forfeit his leadership standing and probably never recover it. Some voiced opposition to Bob's direction. Couldn't he trust God to take care of his needs? But Bob was determined to follow God's direction, even though it meant laying down excellent opportunities for advancement.

Four years later, God has opened new doors for Bob. He is now associate pastor of a growing mainline denominational church, has paid off the debts, and has developed an ever-widening sphere of influence within that group. Bob followed God, even when it looked as if he were being asked to give up the very things for which he had fought and dreamed.

The Bible is much more realistic than we are about the human condition. The prophet Jeremiah informs us that, "The heart is deceitful above all things and beyond cure. Who can understand it?" (Jeremiah 17:9). After dealing with my own deceitfulness for many years, I have come to recognize at least some of the telltale signs that my heart motives are not right. Let me outline four of the most basic:

Name dropping—A person having the compulsion to inform others of such things as the invitations he has received or the "name" people he knows, is deeply insecure. His insecurity will cloud his motives.

Refusal to be checked by others—The person who closes himself off from correction or reproof is determined to run things according to personal desire. He will end up surrounding himself only with those who are blindly loyal.

Vain ambition—The leader beset with this motive is characterized by the need to promote his ministry. People become pawns or "contacts" who are used to further the leader's ministry, credibility, or reputation. Using people in this way is not always a conscious act, but it will undoubtedly surface when one is scrambling frantically to establish a ministry upon the sifting sand of human effort.

Using the end to justify the means—Compromising ethical integrity starts out as just a "small" thing, especially in fiscal matters. Rationalizing the need to "get the message out there," the person suppresses the still small voice of conscience in order to keep the ministry going.

One of the greatest tests for any aspiring servant leader is to walk away from Capernaum as Jesus did. Can we follow His example, or are the hooks of ambition and pride too firmly embedded in us? May our eyes be fixed on Gennesaret and the villages beyond, lest we become entrapped in our Capernaums, unable to disentangle ourselves to do the will of the One who calls us His children.

Chapter Three

Seeing the Potential
(Luke 19)

Nehu hoisted Ezra onto his shoulders. "Can you see now?" he asked, raising his voice above the din of the swelling crowd.

"No, Papa. That fig tree is still in the way," Ezra replied.

Nehu wondered what he should do next. Actually, he would have liked to continue with his work, but that was impossible. He could not understand what all the fuss was really about. So a holy man was coming to town. Holy men were always coming to town. But Nehu had never before had to close his booth because of it. He'd heard snippets of information all morning. This Holy Man apparently could perform great miracles. And even though He wasn't actually a priest or a rabbi, He often read and taught in synagogues.

Nehu let out a sigh of frustration. Why didn't the Man just come to town on the Sabbath? Today was a busy day in the market. Finally, Nehu had to close his booth. The gathering crowd had been packed so tightly in front of the booth that it had been pointless trying to sell any more cloth. And besides, the crowd wanted nothing of any merchant this afternoon. They were waiting expectantly for the Holy Man.

As Nehu turned to move farther down the road, he caught sight of the tax collector. Zacchaeus stood out because he was shorter and wider than anyone else and his apparel was gaudy. Nehu spat on the ground as he felt his contempt rise. Several conspicuous rings glistened on Zacchaeus' fingers, and his stubby bulk was accentuated by the expensive brocade robe encompassing his girth.

Nehu knew it was expensive. It had come from the most exquisite bolt in his stall. He cursed the fact that he had not seen Zacchaeus coming in that day in time to hide his most expensive merchandise. Naturally Zacchaeus had wanted the fabric, and it became obvious that he was not going to leave until he had been "given" a robe's length of the fabric.

Nehu cursed to himself. Was nothing safe anymore? The Romans had done more than rule over the Jews. They had subverted them—Jew against Jew, one man's wits pitted against the next. Even some within one's own household were willing to inform, ready to do the overlord's bidding for small enough reward.

The corners of Nehu's lips curled as he watched Zacchaeus. Perhaps standing too long in the afternoon sun had made the crowd overly bold. It seemed to Nehu that some form of collective drunkenness had come over them as they crudely jostled Zacchaeus.

None of them would have dared touch the chief tax collector normally, but now one person nudged him with his elbow while the next person stuck his foot out to trip him. The crowd would never let Zacchaeus get to any kind of vantage point even remotely suiting either the man's diminutive height or his ego.

Nehu broke into a broad grin as he watched the scene. This was worth half a day's business to see. Finally the tax collector retreated in exasperation, a stormy glare fixed on his face and plans of retribution gathering in his mind.

The pantomime over, Nehu slipped the small child off his shoulders. "We might as well go farther down the road. The whole town seems transfixed with this Man's arrival." They moved along behind the crowd. The heat from the noonday sun intensified. The gentle breeze that had wafted across the town all morning had abated, and now the dust kicked up by the crowd hung like a blanket in the torrid air.

Finally Nehu selected a spot under the shade of a huge sycamore tree from which to view the arrival of the Holy Man. He hoisted his son onto his shoulders and waited. This Man must surely be important, Nehu speculated, as he spotted numerous men of status from the village among the crowd.

Suddenly the crowd erupted. Nehu craned to see over the two women in front of him. The Holy Man was coming. He made His way slowly, stopping now and then to speak with people. Nehu was too far away to hear what He was saying, but there was no hiding the fact that this Holy Man was enormously popular.

As the Holy Man came closer, the sense of excitement in the air captivated Nehu. He found himself anxious to get a good look at this Man.

It was as though someone had read his thoughts. The Holy Man stopped directly in front of Nehu, whose heart skipped a beat. The Man looked into Nehu's eyes for a moment. His eyes were warm and dark and held no malice or hypocrisy. Nehu felt strangely naked and vulnerable in their gaze. Then the Holy Man's gaze shifted to the branches of the tree above Nehu.

"Zacchaeus!"

Nehu turned his head to follow the Holy Man's gaze. Then he saw. Zacchaeus clutched unceremoniously and desperately to one of the lower branches. Nehu was incredulous. Did Zacchaeus have no dignity at all? And how did the Holy Man know his name? Surely He knew of this man's disgusting reputation.

For the second time that day, Nehu waited to see the fat little man be publicly humiliated. This time it was not merely the jostling of a few street merchants, it was the visiting Celebrity Himself who was going to address the pompous Roman sell-out. And again Nehu smiled. He saw it all.

This Holy Man was a brilliant strategist. He had obviously asked someone to go ahead to find out who was the most unpopular man in town. By publicly denouncing that person, He would win many people over instantly.

Nehu waited delightedly. And then the Holy Man spoke. "Zacchaeus, hurry up and come down from your tree. I need to stay at your house tonight."

A murmur of disbelief rippled through the crowd. Eyes darted from the Holy Man to Zacchaeus and back again, searching for meaning in the absurd request. The Holy Man and the tax collector? How could it be?

Quickly, and with surprising agility considering his size, the chief tax collector climbed out of the tree. The crowd parted as the two moved toward each other. A genuine smile of friendship spread across the Holy Man's face as He embraced the short, fat man.

Then unexpectedly, as much as anything could be unexpected at that moment, the tax collector blurted out, "Lord! Here and now I give half of my possessions to the poor, and if I have cheated anybody out of anything, I will pay back four times the amount."

Nehu watched, spellbound, hardly aware of the small child on his shoulders tugging at his hair to get down. Could the tax collector really mean this? What was going on here? Was the Holy Man really going to defile Himself by staying with a traitor? And was Zacchaeus really serious about what he had just said, or had he somehow become deranged?

There was genuine warmth in the Holy Man's face as He spoke respectfully to the tax collector. Or was He really speaking to the crowd? "Today salvation has come to this house, because this man, too, is a son of Abraham. For the Son of Man came to seek and to save what was lost."

Like most of the others, Nehu was still trying to grasp this totally unexpected development when Zacchaeus brushed past him. "Yours will be the first booth I stop at tomorrow. I have a debt to settle. I believe this cloth was very expensive. I shall bring my traveling purse with me." Zacchaeus smiled a simple, transparent smile, completely lacking in guile or sarcasm as far as Nehu could tell.

Somehow as he watched the two make their way down the crowded street, Nehu really believed Zacchaeus would be at his booth tomorrow—but not the same Zacchaeus he had known before.

The attribute of acceptance emanating from the heart of a compassionate leader often becomes the sole means of rescue for the person without hope.

I was recently reading in a newspaper a plea for a particular mainline denomination to ordain homosexual ministers. The man making the plea expressed himself in a letter: "If the Christian church is called to accept others, and to live in harmony as brothers and sisters, then why is it that you so blatantly reject homosexuals? What gives you the right to judge us? The Bible says, 'Judge not lest you yourselves be judged.' Yet we are continually being bombarded by

'Christian' people who reject us without knowing us. Many of us have found love and acceptance in the world. How ironic that we cannot find it within the walls of a church."

Everywhere we go we hear that Christians should love and accept others. I would agree. But accepting others does not mean accepting them with the kind of bland, passive, "anything goes" mentality that the writer of this letter would have us practice. That is not how Jesus accepted Zacchaeus in the vignette above. Jesus accepted Zacchaeus as a person made by God, but certainly did not accept his habits or lifestyle. By His presence Jesus challenged the way Zacchaeus lived. As a result, Zacchaeus willingly offered to change his ways and make restitution to those he had harmed.

I have a six-year-old son, Timmy. I accept Timmy unconditionally. No matter what he does, he will always be my son. If he had been born retarded or handicapped, he would still be my son. If he becomes a criminal, he will still be my son. But although I accept him unconditionally as a person, I do not always accept his behavior. There are times when I have to reprove and correct his behavior in order to help him grow up to be an emotionally healthy and balanced person.

That is what Jesus did for Zacchaeus. He challenged his behavior. I doubt if the challenge stopped with this single encounter under a sycamore tree. I am sure that as Jesus ate with Zacchaeus and slept in his house He motivated him to new levels of behavior. Jesus could do nothing else. To accept Zacchaeus' habits and lifestyle without seeking to help change them would not have been appropriate acceptance but mere tolerance. God, however, does not tolerate sin. He abhors it. Thus Jesus was compelled by the very nature of who He was—the Son of God—to love and accept people as God's unique creation, while at the same time challenging them to repentance, restitution, spiritual growth, and maturity.

The man who wants the church to ordain and accept homosexual ministers wants more than we as Christians are able to offer. We can accept those who live lifestyles contrary to Biblical injunction as human beings and objects of God's love, but we cannot shrink from inciting them to realign their lives according to God's standards.

Jesus did not shirk His responsibility in this regard. He was constantly spurring the disciples to spiritual growth, and it wasn't always comfortable for them. I don't think it was comfortable for Peter when Jesus told him, "Get behind Me, Satan." Or for James and John as Jesus sternly addressed them after their request to sit on either side of Him in heaven.

A word of caution should be added, though. Challenging a person's lifestyle or behavior in the hope of moving them away from sin and on to new levels of spiritual growth in no way justifies using belittling or demeaning conversation on our part. It is not an open door for leaders to verbally pick on those under their leadership, nor does it mean we prophesy their doom if they fail to respond to our challenge. The servant leader's major tool for promoting spiritual growth should be love, not judgment.

In confronting Zacchaeus, Jesus was able to look beyond who he was and see what he could become. A servant leader must choose to look beyond the fractured world of a person's current behavior and focus instead on the potential God has given them. This requires accepting the person, regardless of his behavior. Acceptance of this type is often the key that unlocks the guarded treasure of hidden potential resident in all human hearts.

Perhaps Francois de Fenelon sums it up best:

> Charity does not demand of us that we
> should never see the faults of others; we must,
> in that case, put out our eyes. But it commands
> us to avoid attending unnecessarily to them,
> and that we be not blind to the good, while we
> are so clear-sighted to the evil that exists. We
> ought to remember what God can do from one
> moment to another for the most unworthy crea-
> ture, and think how many causes we have to
> think ill of ourselves, and finally, we must con-
> sider that charity embraces the very lowest. It
> acknowledges that in the sight of God, the con-
> tempt that we indulge for others has in it some-
> thing harsh and arrogant which extinguishes
> the spirit of Jesus Christ.[3]

Recently I visited a ministry where the leader
proudly informed me that he had no difficulties with
anyone on his staff. He assured me he had reached the
grand plateau of accepting every single person in the
ministry as they were. As my visit progressed, we had
a lot of time to talk. It wasn't long before I could see
exactly why he felt he wasn't having any problems or
difficulties with any of his staff. He really did not
know any of them except in a very superficial, work-
related manner. He was not involved in their lives. He
had confused disassociation with acceptance.

As a leader, it is easy to "gloss over" people. It
appears there are no real problems, but that is only
because there is no real involvement in their lives. I
was confronted by this lesson early in my leadership,
and I learned it the hard way.

There was a couple on my staff whom I treated as
acquaintances. I didn't appear to have a lot in common with them, so my wife and I only mixed with

them on a casual social basis. There were times when other members of the ministry tried to tell me the couple was having some problems, but I was too busy and decided to "let sleeping dogs lie."

It wasn't until the couple left the ministry abruptly and filed for divorce that I realized the gravity and seriousness of my mistake. I had not taken the time to involve myself in their lives. I really didn't know the couple beyond the social veneer of casual visits. As their leader, I had accepted them, but had never challenged them. And in practicing the one without the other, I had failed them as their leader.

That which distinguishes biblically appropriate acceptance from unconcerned tolerance is compassion. Compassion, which literally means "to feel pain jointly," is the quality which allows one person to enter into the felt needs of another. It is a deep inner desire to identify with someone else in order to be a compassionate channel of healing to them.

Tolerance, on the other hand, is passive acquiescence, or a state of non-involvement. It is an outward attempt to give credibility to a heart that is inwardly unconcerned. It is sad but true that many in the Church today are tolerated, but few are properly accepted.

With incisive revelation Henri Nouwen puts it this way: "The tragedy of Christian ministry is that many who are in great need, many who seek an attentive ear, a word of support, a forgiving embrace, a firm hand, a tender smile, or even a stuttering confession of inability to do more, often find their ministers distant men who do not want to burn their fingers."[4]

Servant leaders cannot choose whether they will or will not become involved in the lives of those around them. Jesus, the Servant Leader, exemplified involvement in the act of His incarnation. But beyond becoming a man for the sake of identity and involvement, Jesus also became a servant. He "made himself nothing, taking the very nature of a servant" (Philippians 2:7).

While living in Morocco a number of years ago, the real meaning of the incarnation was driven home to me. Many of the wonderful Moroccans we met were Muslims who felt obligated to appease Allah. Unfortunately, they had no way of knowing if they had managed to do enough to satisfy him. Their god required appeasement and performance. In exchange, he offered no hint of involvement or personal care.

One particular day another young man and myself had gone into the *casbah* to go shopping. Just before entering the open vegetable market, we were accosted by a teen-aged Moroccan. In fluent English he asked us if we were "Jesus people." We told him we were. He then requested that we come into his souvenir shop and talk to his uncle about God. Not yet familiar with the local culture, we went inside, thinking how nice of the Lord to give us this easy opportunity to share our faith.

Inside, the teenager introduced us to his uncle, who, he explained, could not speak English. The uncle, a pleasant smile on his face, ushered us to a couple of chairs placed against the back wall of the shop. In Arabic, he then asked, "What is the name of your god?" The nephew interpreted the question into English, then gave our reply to his uncle.

Next, the uncle asked us if our God had a Son and if so, what was His name? As soon as I spoke the name of Jesus, this pleasant Arab gentleman exploded in anger, and in very articulate English informed us that we had just endeavored to proselytize him. Therefore, he was going to send his nephew for the police and we would be arrested for attempting to convert a

Muslim. Speaking in Arabic, the man then commanded his nephew to find the police and bring them to the shop.

I looked at my friend in disbelief as nightmares of spending the rest of my life in prison came to mind. My friend's face portrayed the panic I felt. Not particularly being in the mood to become a martyr, I hissed, "Let's get out of here!"

What followed would surely have made a great scene in a Laurel and Hardy movie, though I failed to see the humor at the time. As we started to walk around the man to get to the front door, he jumped upon my friend's back and held on with grim determination, all the while yelling at the top of his voice about Allah's justice for infidels.

I tried to grab the man from behind to pry him off my friend, but the man would not budge. In the process of this unlikely wrestling match, we had dragged ourselves across the shop to the front door. At the doorway, the man began to yell for help at the top of his lungs.

Twenty yards down the narrow street was the open market, mobbed by customers. Many were men. They all looked to my fearful eyes like giants, and those giants headed toward us. Now I knew for sure that the end was near.

Panic-stricken, we froze, trying our best to assure everyone that we meant no harm. Several men from the crowd surrounded us. The shop owner crawled off my friend's back. We tried to reason with the man, but he wouldn't listen.

After what seemed an eternity, the nephew came running up to the shop, out of breath. "Uncle," he gasped, "I have run throughout the *casbah* and I cannot find any policemen."

"That's strange," muttered the uncle. *It certainly is,*

I thought to myself. Normally there were policemen everywhere.

"That's all right," snapped the uncle. "We shall close the shop and escort them to the police station ourselves." At that, the man turned to lock the shop door. As he did, his nephew leaned over and whispered in my ear, "You guys run for it. I'll keep my uncle from following."

Needing no further encouragement, we bolted through the startled onlookers with terror-stricken haste and ran until we literally dropped from exhaustion. It was soon apparent that our superior speed, grace, and athleticism, fueled by gigantic amounts of fear, had distanced us from danger.

A local British doctor later informed us that the man was undoubtedly on a quest to appease Allah. He thought he could earn valuable merit points by framing a Christian infidel.

The point of the episode is that this man was so obsessed with his attempt to gain the favor of his god that he was more than willing to set aside friendly discussion in favor of entrapment. We have all met born-again believers who do the same.

The God of the Bible stands in stark contrast to this. He does not ask to be appeased in the way this man attempted to appease Allah. Quite the opposite. He sent His Son into the world in the form of a servant to serve mankind. And He committed Himself to ultimate involvement in people's lives by allowing Jesus to die on the cross that we might be made acceptable to Him.

As servant leaders, are we conduits of these qualities which God has modeled for us through His Son? Or are we like the gods of other religions? Are we unaware of and uninvolved in the lives of those we lead? Do our followers have to appease us in order to stay on our good side? Do we display disgust and disappointment when our followers do not perform to our expectations?

Acceptance, involvement, and *challenge* are three words which are indispensable in,the vocabulary of the servant leader. But they are more than words. They are attributes that flow daily from the servant leader's life to those he leads as he draws them on to new levels of spiritual growth and maturity.

Chapter Four

Partial Treatment
(Matthew 20)

Salome placed the last of her dried fish in the basket along with the bread and the grapes, smiling in satisfaction as she did so. It would be enough food for the entire group to eat well. It was the last of her dried fish, and now that her sons were with the Master most of the time, she wasn't sure when there would be more fish to dry to replenish her stock. She didn't really mind. Salome was shrewd enough to know that short-term sacrifices were sometimes required to attain long-term security.

Everything was going according to plan. She pulled the door shut and made her way toward the northern quarter of the city. Her new white robe gleamed in the bright midday sun, and tendrils of black hair peeked from the edge of her scarf. She had taken extra care in grooming herself this morning.

She walked a mile before she spotted the group. They were just entering the house of Zadok. *Good*, she thought to herself. *They are retiring together for a rest. The Master will be relaxed, and there will be no one else to distract Him.* She quickened her pace and arrived at Zadok's door just as the servant was about to close it.

"My sons—I have come to see my sons," she said, glancing down at the basket. The elderly servant gave

a toothless smile as he admitted her into the courtyard.

Almost twenty men milled around in the courtyard. She could see her sons talking energetically to a
burly, rough-hewn fellow.

He must be the one they call "The Rock," she thought,
recalling her son's description of him. She moved
closer. The Rock looked likable enough, but her sons
had told her that the Master found him impetuous and
had had to rebuke him on a number of occasions,
sometimes in public.

A surge of satisfaction ran through her as she
thought of the Master rebuking this hulk of a man. It
would never be necessary for Him to rebuke her sons.
She had raised her sons better than that. And if the
Master agreed, her efforts were going to be rewarded.
Indeed, her sons were already well thought of by the
Master. It was said that her eldest son held a special
place in the Master's heart.

As she approached, the Rock and her two sons
turned to welcome her. The basket she was carrying
made her doubly welcome. Her boys knew it undoubtedly held some of the delectable dried fish their
mother was renowned for.

Salome greeted each of her sons. They couldn't
help but notice her preoccupation as she distractedly
studied the courtyard beyond them. Her eyes darted
back and forth, fixing the scene in her mind. It was as
she imagined it would be. Some of the men were
reclining, others were drawing water and drinking
from two large earthen jars at the back of the courtyard. The atmosphere was relaxing and calm—a perfect atmosphere in which to carry out their plan.

Salome motioned for her sons to come closer and
then she whispered, "Now's the right time. I will do
the talking."

John looked a little uncomfortable. He would have preferred a more private place, but knew better than to challenge his mother. And it had been his and James' idea in the first place, so they'd better be prepared to carry it through. They followed their mother as she made her way toward the Master. He was alone, leaning against the wall at the side of the courtyard.

Salome had practiced this moment a thousand times in her mind. She knew what to do. Demurely, she approached the Master, eyes lowered, arms extended, offering the basket of food.

"Master," she began in a clear and confident voice, "I have brought this food for the sustenance of You and Your disciples."

The Master focused His attention on her, "Thank you. The Father will reward you for your kindness."

Salome placed the basket at the Master's feet and knelt down in front of Him. The Master picked up the basket and motioned for one of His disciples to come and take it from Him. For a moment, John wanted to run. The plan they had devised seemed so tacky now.

The Master looked down at Salome. "What is it you want?" He asked in a soft and guileless tone. For a moment she felt reluctant to go on. Then the calming security of being flanked by her two sons restored her confidence. What she was about to ask for was on their behalf.

Salome stammered out the first few words as she collected herself, scrambling for the safety of her memorized request. "Grant that one of these two sons of mine may sit at Your right and the other at Your left in Your Kingdom." The anxiety of the moment had propelled the words from her mouth with a little more forcefulness than she had intended.

The Master's eyes were fixed firmly upon her, and the light of understanding shone brightly in them. He shifted His weight and looked at the two sons standing on either side of their mother.

"You don't know what you are asking, woman." He turned His attention to James and John and asked, "Can you drink the cup I am going to drink?"

"Of course we can," the two brothers mumbled in unison, not exactly sure they understood the question, but eager to meet the Master's prerequisites for power.

"You know that the Gentile rulers lord it over their people." The Master's eyes stared directly, piercingly into the eyes of James and John.

"We already know all that..." James blurted out, a sense of frustration in his voice. Things were not going quite as planned.

"It is not that way among you." The Master's words sliced across their consciousness. "Whoever wants to become great among you must be your servant."

They were speechless, stunned at the Master's choice of words.

The Master continued on: "Just as the Son of Man did not come to be served, but to serve."

In an instant John saw it. The Master was right. He had never exercised His power over them. What arrogance it was to presume that the Master would now begin to rank them over each other. Tears sprung to John's eyes as the revelation hit him.

"Forgive us," John spoke with quiet urgency as he helped his mother to her feet. The Master acknowledged John's request and left them to ponder what He had said.

The two boys silently escorted their mother to the entrance of Zadok's house. She had so many thoughts to sort through. Weren't her sons following the Man who would soon overthrow the Romans and restore peace and honor to Israel? She had willingly sacrificed her sons' livelihood to that end. Didn't the Master owe them something in return?

Salome's shoulders were hunched in confused disappointment as she spoke her farewells. As James and John turned back to the group, the Rock yelled to them: "Tell your mother she's welcome anytime. This fish is great!"

The temptation to gain special favor or to extend partial treatment can only weave its seductive spell upon the soul impressed with status.

James and John, along with their mother, were caught off guard by Jesus' response to Salome's request for special treatment. All their arguments were quelled as He said, "The Son of Man did not come to be served, but to serve." That simple statement left them no room to maneuver. If Jesus declined to acknowledge His own status, there was no chance He was going to confer status on them.

How different the Kingdom of God is from the kingdoms of this world! The great Servant Leader refused to entertain notions of exercising His status for personal prestige. Neither would He play favorites. He knew, as the Psalmist knew, that advancement comes from neither the east or west, but from God, and that the servant leader must choose the path of downward mobility.[5]

"God is no respecter of persons." We know these words as well as we know our own names. Yet in the routine of daily events, leaders are often predisposed toward selective partiality in their relationships. Thus every leader must often ask himself the following questions. "Do people with perceived status receive special attention from me? Do I 'turn on' charm and kindness in the presence of those from whom I want or need something? Am I quick to remind people of my own status?" For many of us, I suspect, the answer to these questions is "yes."

Leadership in today's fallen world is often understood as upward advancement. This view encourages the seductive magnetism of being "over" others, and this magnetism exerts a compelling force upon the hearts of men. Few leaders can resist being seduced by it, and, having once tasted, few are willing to relinquish the addictive pull of the status and power which come through position.

My first awareness of the deception of status and partiality occurred when I was nineteen years old. I accompanied my father to an annual pastor's conference. I felt very comfortable at the first meeting. I knew most of the pastors present. A number of them had stayed in our home over the years.

After one of the evening services, we headed for a nearby restaurant which had become the unofficial place to congregate during the conference. As we sat together in the restaurant, my teenaged mind was confronted with a startling revelation.

Pastors who had been so friendly when they were guests in our home now seemed barely civil toward my father. It took no genius to quickly recognize that the unfriendly pastors were generally those who pastored churches larger than the one my father pastored. These pastors, I'm sure unconsciously, clustered together in cliques away from the others. The pastors of medium-sized churches also sat together in groups. I looked around the restaurant and could not see any pastors from the denomination's smaller churches.

Status is such a blind spot for us of the evangelical church in the western world. We castigate, and rightfully so, the inescapable caste systems of India. Yet our own culture wraps its capitulation to status around us in such subtle ways that we deny its reality and its hold on our thinking.

I recently attended a wedding reception that was also attended by some so-called big name people of the evangelical church world. I felt embarrassed as the reception progressed, watching supposedly mature adults jockey for position, vying for the attention of the celebrities in the room. I have watched the same phenomenon occur at major Christian conventions, where status was conferred in proportion to the size of entourage following in the wake of the "super star" of the moment.

Jesus deplored categorizing people according to "worldly importance," and refused to have anything to do with such a charade. His responses to the Samaritan woman at the well were as sincere and caring as His responses to the wealthy and powerful men with whom He came in contact. Status, whether His own or that of others, meant nothing to Jesus. For Him, *agape* love was something to bestow freely upon all men, not just upon those holding places of prominence.

"Lisa" is a vibrant and talented woman who serves with Youth With A Mission. She recently shared with me how when she began serving with the mission, she was a worker in the housekeeping department at one of our large ministry centers overseas. During those early days, she felt lonely and isolated.

Another American woman, the wife of one of the leaders, supervised the housekeeping department. Lisa tried to reach out to her for friendship and support. Alas, this other woman seemed to have time for nothing but the most cursory of remarks.

Ten years later, Lisa and the leader's wife met at a large international conference. By that time Lisa had found her niche and had become well known. During one of the sessions at the conference, Lisa was introduced to the gathered crowd. The leader's wife came to her afterward, chuckled nervously, and said, "You know, you look so familiar. I can't quite place you. You look like someone I had cleaning for me at one of our centers, but that's ridiculous." She chuckled again.

Lisa looked into the eye of the person she had wanted as a friend and replied, "No, it's not ridiculous. That's exactly where we met. You were supervisor of the housekeeping department." The woman became flustered and soon excused herself from the conversation.

Why is it so ridiculous to think that a person could be cleaning toilets one day and have an important ministry the next, or vice versa? We have let so much of the world's way of categorizing people creep into our own hearts. I hope that woman left the meeting realizing the shallowness of her commitment to a sister in the Lord.

Preparation for ruling and reigning with Christ does not begin with ruling and reigning. It begins with service. If in the course of our service God should place us in a position of leadership, it is imperative that we not consider menial and mundane tasks beneath our dignity.

Richard Foster states it well: "The ministry of small things must be prior to and more valued than the ministry of power. Without this perspective we will view power as a 'big deal.' Make no mistake, the religion of the 'big deal' stands in opposition to the way of Christ."[6]

The leader who only wants to do "big things" for God reveals the true nature of his motives. "There is no real elevation of mind in a contempt of little things; it is, on the contrary, from too narrow views that we consider those things of little importance, which have in fact such extensive consequences."[7]

The true servant leader views no person as incidental, nor does he believe in "chance meetings." Each engagement with another person is seen as an opportunity to express Christlikeness with no preference given because of status, position, race, gender, or denominational affiliation.

Jesus made truth, not position, the foundation of His authority. He made decisions because He was, and is, the truth. And authority from the biblical perspective continues to be based in truth and righteousness, not natural ability, wealth, or position.

Leaders attracted by position soon expose themselves by their partiality and favoritism. James, however, tells us succinctly: "My brothers, as believers in our glorious Lord Jesus Christ, don't show favoritism" (James 2:1). Further on in the same chapter he makes the point that partiality is a violation of the royal law of love (James 2:8-9). James then sums things up by listing the traits of heavenly wisdom in James 3:17: "But the wisdom that comes from heaven is first of all pure; then peace loving, considerate, submissive, full of mercy and good fruit, impartial and sincere."

Our relationships with each other must always override our status. Only when we cease being enamored with our status will we be able to respond to others impartially.

James and John sought positions of status. They desired to be elevated to a place of prestige where they could lord it over those around them. Jesus lovingly pointed out the folly of their request. In so doing, He pointed them to a higher way, the way of the Kingdom of God. That way was service. He who would be great must be the servant of all.

By humbly choosing to serve behind the scenes,

doing the things that others avoid doing, we are in no way negating our leadership call or gift. Rather we are strengthening it by recognizing that no one is so great that certain tasks are beneath their dignity.

Servanthood is the antidote for status, and it is the opposite of the corporate leadership structure which has invaded today's Church. The aspiring servant leader must follow in the footsteps of the Master, not the steps that lead to the top of the corporate status ladder. Again, the words of Richard Foster are so appropriate: "Servant leaders are people who are servants before they are leaders and will be servants when the tenure of leadership is concluded."[8]

Chapter Five

Open to Others
(Luke 7)

Simon of Bethany greeted the Teacher at the entrance to his palatial home. The rings on his fingers glittered in the midday sun. Simon's greeting was purposely reserved as he motioned the Teacher inside.

He kept his eyes diverted from the large brass basin at the door. Normally he would have called his servant to wash a guest's feet, and he had debated whether he should do it for the Teacher. Finally he had decided against it. He wasn't sure that it was fit for him, a Pharisee, to honor the Teacher in that way. He didn't want to give the Teacher the wrong idea.

The Teacher was a man of mediocre heritage from Nazareth. Simon was curious to learn more about the Teacher's claims, but on his own terms. He did not want it to be thought that he was giving the Teacher any form of endorsement.

Still, as he walked past the empty basin, he could not help but feel uncomfortable. Thankfully, the Teacher did not appear to notice anything out of the ordinary, and soon they were seated together at the table.

Simon surveyed the meal with a sense of satisfaction. Each dish, meticulously prepared, spoke of his status. It pleased him greatly, and he wondered if the

Teacher realized how lucky He was to be a guest in this home.

An awkward silence fell between the two men as they began eating. Simon began to wonder why he had invited the Teacher at all, since He seemed almost oblivious to the honor of being in the home of one of the wealthiest and most influential men in town. What had he really wanted to ask the Teacher? He wasn't sure anymore.

Then they heard the sound of scuffling feet behind them. Simon assumed it to be an over-zealous servant bringing the next course before they were finished eating the first. Without turning to acknowledge the servant, Simon raised his hand as a signal to stop him. Perplexed when the noise of the scuffling footsteps did not recede, he turned only to see a woman who had no place being in his home.

Loathing convulsed Simon as he recognized the woman. He had seen her many times waiting outside the west gate, vying for customers. This whore was in his house. How did she get in? What did she want?

Before Simon could decide how to deal with the situation, the woman stopped in front of the Teacher. She knelt at his feet and drew an alabaster flask from beneath her tunic. She placed the flask beside His feet and looked up into the Teacher's eyes.

The apprehension etched upon her once-beautiful face was met with compassion on His. She buried her head in her hands and cried uncontrollably.

Simon immediately beckoned for a servant. This was outrageous! It was meant to be a private dinner, and now a prostitute was turning it into a fiasco! Simon beckoned again, his irritation deepening.

He glanced at his Guest. How embarrassed the Teacher must feel. But when Simon looked closely at His face, he was puzzled. He didn't know how to interpret the expression on the Teacher's face.

The prostitute loosened the stopper on the flask and began pouring its contents over the Teacher's feet. Tears and oil mingled as she massaged His feet. Normally, her action would have appeared sensuous, but this time, it seemed more like an act of worship.

The woman reached up and unfastened her hair clasp. Her long, black hair tumbled free. She lowered her head and began wiping the oil and tears from the Teacher's feet with her hair.

Now Simon was furious! First, this woman had the gall to enter his home uninvited. Second, the Teacher was undoubtedly a fraud. He, Simon, had been fooled into entertaining a fraud! A man with any spiritual discernment, and certainly one who paraded around as the Son of God, would know that it was a prostitute who was groveling at His feet.

Simon was still scowling when the Teacher turned to him. "Do you see this woman? I came into your house. You did not give Me any water for My feet, but she wet My feet with her tears and wiped them with her hair. You did not give Me a kiss, but this woman, from the time she entered, has not stopped kissing My feet. You did not put oil on My head, but she has poured perfume on My feet. Therefore, I tell you, her many sins have been forgiven—for she loved much."

Simon seethed with anger and embarrassment. His Guest was clearly inferring that this woman had shown more hospitality than he had. It was an outrage, an insult! He was in his own home, and the Teacher was making him feel like a sinner.

The leader willing to receive ministry from a follower— be it encouragement, correction, or instruction—places himself in the grand lineage of those persons worthy to be called disciples.

I'm sure that many of us have been around leaders who have the imperious air of being unapproachable. By mannerisms and actions they project a studied aura of spirituality. They want others to know how special they are. While they may use the language of servanthood, they always place themselves in a position where only they can minister. They may receive ministry from others, but only from those of similar rank and maturity, and certainly not from those "below" them!

Simon would have fit in this mold. However, as we see in the vignette, Jesus refused to be impressed by him. Despite the fact that Simon had invited Jesus into his house as a guest, he remained closed off from Him. He was unsure of Jesus' real stature as a leader and certainly wasn't going to open up and receive from Him until he was sure that Jesus was at least an equal.

Jesus would have none of it. Instead, He reacted in the opposite attitude. He allowed a well-known prostitute to minister to Him. Simon had neglected the most basic of courtesies upon Jesus' arrival at his house. But this prostitute eagerly ministered to Jesus' need, and He willingly received it.

Often we think of Jesus as continually giving out to people. We forget that He also often received ministry from others. Luke tells us: "The Twelve were with him, and also some women who had been cured of evil spirits and diseases: Mary (called Magdalene) from whom seven demons had come out; Joanna the wife of Cuza, the manager of Herod's household; Susanna; and many others. These women were helping to support them out of their own means" (Luke 8:1-3).

Unfortunately, it is the tendency of many spiritual leaders today to view only one side of the coin with regard to ministry. Jesus taught that it is better to give than to receive. But our egotistical interpretation of this in relation to leadership and ministry often blinds us to the fact that we need the humility to graciously receive ministry from others, even from those whom we feel have not achieved our level of maturity. The carnal leader detests the appearance of being either in a subordinate position, or in a place of need when surrounded by subordinates.

Please note that the word *subordinate* has no place in the language of the Kingdom. I use it here merely to emphasize that leaders need to be secure enough to switch roles with those they view as "under" them.

On the other hand, a servant leader understands that he, in common with all humanity, stands in the place of need. In addition, he recognizes that humbly receiving ministry from a subordinate actually allows the subordinate to grow in confidence. Thus, unconcerned with image, the servant leader willingly places himself in situations of need or subordination in order that the one meeting his need may blossom as a leader in his own right.

"Frank" was a self-sufficient person, a pastor with a happy family and a growing ministry. As far as I could tell from the outside, everything was falling into place for him. Yet Frank had called me over to talk. Something was troubling him. I sat across the desk from Frank in his study.

We chatted glibly for a few minutes until Frank finally took a deep breath and said, "I don't think I can take it any more. I don't know why I ever went into the ministry in the first place." He stopped to gauge my reaction. I tried not to show any.

"The other day I was given a couple of tickets to a ball game," he continued, "and I wanted to take a buddy with me. Do you know, I couldn't think of anyone to take! Sure, there are a lot of people who do what I tell them to, but I don't have a single friend—

someone I can talk to, someone I can share my problems with." I nodded sympathetically, having felt the same way at times myself.

Frank continued, "It never used to be this way. In college and when I was first married, I used to have lots of friends. But since I became a pastor, nobody wants to spend time with me any more."

As the conversation progressed, we pinpointed the source of Frank's loneliness. He had fallen into the same trap so many other Christian leaders have fallen into. He had put himself "above" his congregation and no longer felt he was able to be himself around them. He now had an image to protect.

What would the congregation do if they knew he lost his temper at his teenage son, or if they knew he was not as regular as he should be in prayer and Bible study? He felt others would not look up to him if he did not protect the "image" of his leadership.

Yet exactly the opposite is true. Nobody wants to spend time with a person who is projecting an image rather than sharing his life with them. Most of us would rather have a leader who is flawed, but real, than one who is glossy, but phony.

Even Jesus had times of admitted weakness. Consider the time when He was about to be crucified. He prayed, "If it is possible, may this cup be taken from Me." In today's language He may well have said something like: "I really don't want to go through with this. I'm scared and alone. Isn't there any other way?" Jesus was displaying vulnerability, not failure.

Perhaps the most painful thing about Frank's situation was that he had done exactly what he had been trained to do. Many leaders are taught in Bible school and seminary the dictum that good leaders keep a distance between themselves and their followers. This rationale is based upon a military concept of leadership, and has no basis in New Testament thought or practice. Sad to say, most Bible colleges persist in teaching this concept to prospective pastors.

Unfortunately, many of these leaders, like Frank, come to a point in their leadership tenure where they are bereft of both position and friends. How ironic that those who should be most open are often unapproachable.

As Gayle Erwin puts it: "In our society (church and secular), the higher you go up the ladder, the more inaccessible you are to people—the more hidden your personal life is."[9]

The servant leader is willing to expose his humanity, along with all his fears and failings. He realizes that his followers are ultimately not to look to him as their leader, but to the one true leader—Christ.

The need to look impressive is not a part of the thinking of the servant leader, so he is willing to walk the risky road of vulnerability, knowing that the rewards far outweigh the risks.

Do you shield yourself from relationships out of fear? Has your leadership position become a fortress? "Much Christian leadership is exercised by people who do not know how to develop healthy, intimate relationships and have opted for power and control instead."[10] Control is a cheap and exploitative substitute for relationship, and needs to be renounced.

True, it is our weakness that causes us to fail, but it is an even greater weakness to cover up our failings. We must learn to accept ourselves and each other in our "weakened" human state.

Loneliness in leadership is a sign that we have isolated ourself from others, often out of a sense of superiority that causes us to deny not only our weakness, but ultimately, our humanity.

How wonderful that Jesus did not succumb to this

kind of superficial role-playing. In fact, He gracefully submitted to the impulsive act of a harlot who drenched His feet in perfumed oil.

Gayle Erwin makes another convincing statement which applies here: "When Jesus alludes to submission, it is always directed toward leaders or the ones who want to be great in the kingdom and they are always ordered to submit downward, not upward."[11]

The New Testament focus in regard to the relationship of leaders and followers is not primarily on followers obeying leaders. It is on leaders being a living demonstration of what they are teaching.

The weight of responsibility in the leader-follower dynamic tips to the side of the leader, not the follower. Followers inherently understand this. They want to learn from the example of their leaders.

How sad that many leaders, forgetting that they were once followers, place the bulk of responsibility back upon the follower. Countless horror stories now abound in the Body of Christ of followers who have been bludgeoned by the word *submit*.[12] If spiritual leaders would only understand that submission is reciprocal, flowing downward as well as upward, such carnage could easily be avoided.

We each need to evaluate ourselves in this regard. When was the last time that we truly shared our heart, our frustrations, and our dreams with someone in our charge? When was the last time we deliberately put ourselves in a position where we would have to submit to the authority of someone who is normally "ranked" under us?

If we take the time to be open with those around us, if we own up to our humanity and all its attendant weaknesses, if we are willing to lay aside our "reputation and image" in order to follow the Master's example, then we will truly experience a revolution in our leadership. Free from pretension, we will see people rally to us because they can see in us both their reflection and the reflection of the Master. And such a reflection generates hope in the heart of the follower.

The Church has too many leaders cast in the mold of Simon. It is time for the mold to be broken. It is time for a leadership style to come forth that emphasizes openness and humility.

Chapter Six

No Compromise
(Luke 18)

A cold winter wind hurled tiny needles of sand against them. The huddled figures on the narrow road leading from the village winced as the full force of the blustering wind engulfed them. It was the Teacher and His disciples retreating from a village still buzzing with animated fervor at what they had seen and heard. In the midst of the distracted excitement, the Teacher had slipped quietly away.

Judas was used to it by now. He used to get extremely angry when the Teacher retreated from activity, but now, like the others, he'd learned to accept it.

As they walked on, Judas was oblivious to the gathering wind around them, his mind caught up with the fact that they had left town so hurriedly that there hadn't been time to buy food for the journey. And even if there had been time, there wasn't enough money in the purse to pay for it.

The situation frustrated Judas greatly. Things seemed so disorganized around the Teacher. Here they were, heading off into the surrounding countryside with no food or money. If they had stayed a little longer in the village they would surely have been invited to eat at someone's home.

But it was always like this. The Teacher seemed

oblivious to their real needs. Sometimes Judas felt like shaking Him and telling Him to wake up. But Judas just followed along, a sea of frustration tinged with bitterness swirling inside him.

The group did not realize it, but as they receded into the flying dust, someone was watching them. The observer's face would have stood out in any crowd—handsome and bearing the unmistakable lines of wealth, self-confidence, and aristocracy. Beyond the luxurious cape and opulently bejeweled fingers, confusion lingered in the watcher's eyes as he saw the Teacher depart.

"Sir, sir!" he yelled after the group in a vain hope to be heard. He was used to people scurrying to obey his every word. But the Teacher kept walking, and the wind threw the man's words back in his face. He began running after the Teacher, his body straining against the steady head wind.

"Sir!" he called again as he got closer. At last the Teacher heard him. He turned and waited for the young man to catch up. The Teacher recognized him as the rich-looking young man who had been lingering at the edge of the crowd in the village.

Stumbling awkwardly, the young man fell on his knees before the Teacher. "Good teacher," he panted, "what must I do to inherit eternal life?"

Judas and Peter exchanged glances. Why couldn't this man have asked his question earlier in the village instead of waiting until they were on the road in the midst of a gathering storm? Judas felt the exasperation once again. If they had stayed in the village a little longer, this rich-looking young man would surely have invited them to dine with him.

The Teacher placed His hands on the young man's shoulders and looked deeply into his eyes. "Why do you call Me good? No one is good—except God alone." The rich young man nodded, lowering his gaze to the ground. He knew the implications of the Teacher's statement.

"You know the commandments: 'Do not commit adultery, do not murder, do not steal, do not give false testimony, honor your father and mother," the Teacher continued.

"All these I have kept since I was a boy," the young man replied, a hint of frustration in his voice. He had always followed the priest's requirements, but still something was missing. Something vital. He had hoped the Teacher could point out what it was.

Suddenly the potential of the situation dawned upon Judas and brought a smile to his face. This was better than anything he could have planned. Here was what appeared to be an extraordinarily rich young man snivelling at Jesus' feet, begging for instruction on how to receive eternal life.

All the Teacher needed to do was say the word and Judas was sure the man would collect his belongings and join the group. Their penny-pinching days would be over. This man would be able to furnish the money to meet the group's needs, and they would never lack for anything again.

This was their God-given opportunity. Judas only hoped the Teacher had the common sense to see it for what it was and offer the invitation. Sometimes, though, the Teacher was so naive, so witless about these things that Judas decided he had better seize the moment.

"Teacher," Judas said as he stepped in beside Him. "Could I talk to You now? Alone? It's a matter of some urgency."

The Teacher turned and looked at him. It was a look that would have turned away a less determined person. "It will only take a moment," Judas countered.

With a sigh, the Teacher turned back to the rich young man. "You still lack one thing." The young man looked up expectantly. At last, here was the missing link in his quest for righteousness. "Sell everything you have...." Judas whispered a silent prayer of relief and thanks. "...and give it to the poor, and you will have treasure in heaven. Then come, follow Me."

Bewilderment and anguish registered simultaneously...on two faces!

The combining of personal need with ministry function is not only highly suspicious, it is a combustible mixture.

Jesus' refusal to take advantage of an impressionable, rich young man serves as a stunning reminder that purity and integrity in the heart of a man will forbid him from manipulating the message of the Kingdom of God for personal gain.

The servant leader is obligated by his purity of motive to detach his personal financial comfort from all ministry situations. The rapid increase of financial impropriety—subtle in development but devastating in effect—has been the devil's strategic weapon in ambushing countless leaders. Sad to say, some prominent Christian leaders of our day have found that the soil of financial compromise has rapidly turned to quicksand.

The degree of trust conferred upon a leader by a follower often provides situations which the leader can easily exploit to his private advantage. In our story, the perpetual financial needs of the disciples could easily have justified taking advantage of the rich young man's wealth—but only from man's microscopic perspective.

Numerous daily opportunities are presented to Christian leaders to minister to people while at the same time acquiring gain either for themselves or for their ministry. Once a leader surrenders to this temptation and begins to justify his self-serving action, a deadly new factor has been released upon him—the dominating spirit of mammon. Richard Foster says it this way:

> When the Bible refers to money as a power, it does not mean something vague or impersonal. Nor does it mean power in the sense we mean when we speak, for example, of "purchasing power." No, according to Jesus and all the writers of the New Testament, behind money are very real spiritual forces that energize it and give it a life of its own. Hence, money is an active agent; it is a law unto itself; and it is capable of inspiring devotion.[13]

The power of mammon was much in evidence at a Christian social function I once attended. In the crowd were a number of wealthy Christian businessmen. It was painfully embarrassing to watch several ministry leaders—who needed money to support their ministries—come on like debutantes at a charm school as they attempted to impress these wealthy businessmen. It is one thing to directly and humbly request financial aid; it is quite another to manipulatively use "ministry" or flattery as a means to financial gain.

The apostle Paul was very aware of the potential to muddy the waters between ministry and personal gain. J. Oswald Sanders makes the following observation of Paul:

> Paul was very conscious of this ubiquitous problem, and was therefore scrupulous in his financial dealings and his stewardship. In order to remove from the young churches the burden of his support, he earned his own living, and at times he supported his colleagues

as well. He was "financially clean," setting a
noble example of generosity.[14]

It would be easy at this point to launch into a study
of money from a biblical perspective. If we did, we
would discover some interesting things that would
challenge our understanding of money. These things
stand in sharp contrast to the underlying suppositions
of our consumer-driven, debt-ridden society. This
chapter, however, is about motives, not money,
though how we use and think about money tells us
much about our heart motives.

There is no recorded instance of Jesus directing a
person under His authority to give anything to Him,
not even food or money. Jesus' motivation was love
and compassion. He wanted people to understand
what the Kingdom of God was really like so they
could then live their lives in a way that was pleasing
to God. Lives touched and changed were the valida-
tion of His ministry, not the accumulation of personal
power and wealth.

Many of today's spiritual leaders go astray at this
point. After decades of exposure to the consumer
mentality which now defines contemporary America,
some Christians have adapted their theology to ac-
commodate it, resulting in some strange aberrations.

One of these is the notion that material blessing is
a sign of spiritual strength. Thus, the more opulent a
leader's lifestyle is, the more evidence it is to the
faithful that God has truly blessed him and that he
surely must possess a spiritual strength that elevates
him to near sainthood.

This attitude has been elevated to an art form in
some media-driven ministries. The faithful tune in
daily to hear their favorite "saint" deliver his message
which ties together religion and materialism, resulting in gain for his "ministry." They are so blinded by

the notion that material blessing denotes spiritual strength and favor from God that they have never stopped to question motives. They may never question motives until the dirty linen of wrong motives has been hung out by the secular media for all to see. The devastating consequence is that instantly the motives of the most godly leaders are called into question and every spiritual leader is seen by the media through scandal-shaded glasses.

"No one can serve two masters. Either he will hate the one and love the other, or he will be devoted to the one and despise the other. You cannot serve both God and Money" (Matthew 6:24). This was Jesus' summation of the matter. If we are to be servant leaders of Christ, we must deal ruthlessly with the motivations of our heart, especially in the area of our attachment to mammon. To fail to do so is to stray from the path so clearly laid out by our Lord. As recent events have shown, the results of straying from His path are devastation and ruin for the leader and for his followers.

Chapter Seven

Do As I Have Done
(John 13)

Peter entered the room, breathless and late. He had gone to the market to buy bread for the supper and it had taken him longer than expected.

The room was as he had hoped. Sarah, the wife of a wealthy trader, had a comfortable home. It was not opulent, but was richly furnished with many foreign items her husband had traded. Peter smiled to himself. This was more like it. At last things were beginning to come together for the group.

Peter had started out with such high hopes. The Master had healed people, cast out demons, and talked of a new Kingdom that was coming.

But over the last six months it seemed that things had begun to taper off. A subtle change had come over the Master. There was more talk about counting the cost and serving others, but not nearly the number of miracles as at first. Peter had found it a little disturbing, but now he saw it was part of the training. The Master had been testing their loyalty, making sure they were ready. They had to pass through this phase before the "good things" began—and they had begun!

Nothing else in Peter's life compared to the feeling of strutting beside the Master as they entered Jerusalem. He had relived the experience repeatedly in his mind. The frenzy of the people clamoring to lay down their robes in front of the Master, the children ripping branches from nearby palm trees to wave exuberantly at them. And the way the crowd shouted, "Hosanna! Blessed is He who comes in the name of the Lord, even the King of Israel." Yes, Peter reminded himself, they were shouting "King." Finally the Master's obscurity was over; His reign about to begin.

Peter surveyed the room. These were the twelve men the Master was going to take with Him to the top, and Peter, a fisherman, was one of them. Those who had served others were now about to be served. It was perfect, better than Peter could have wished if he had planned it himself.

He placed the bread next to the other food on the table and sat down beside James. "There's plenty more where that came from," he said, sinking into the luxurious red cushion. "As soon as the baker realized I was with the Master, he wouldn't hear of taking payment for the bread. He even said we could come back any time for more and he wouldn't charge us. That's the way it will be from now on. Everyone wants to be in the Master's favor. They're calling Him the next King of Israel, you know?" Peter smiled broadly. Ah yes, things were looking bright!

Peter ate heartily as the conversation continued around him. Some were talking about the authoritative way the Master had overturned the trading tables in the court of the Gentiles. Others were making plans for the future now that the tide had turned for them.

Unnoticed in the midst of the hubbub, the Master rose and made His way out of the room. He reappeared several minutes later, His chest bare and a towel wrapped around His waist. Walking deliberately over to the corner, He poured fresh water into a clay basin. As the Master picked up the basin, an abrupt silence fell on the group.

Peter wondered what the Master was doing now. He looked for all the world like a common servant. The Master knelt in front of Judas and motioned for him to place his foot in the basin. Judas looked terribly uncomfortable as the Master began to wash his feet. As the Master continued, Judas' discomfort turned almost to agitation.

All eyes in the room were fixed on the Master. What was this all about? They watched Him pour a dipper of water over Judas' feet and then tenderly wipe them dry with the towel wrapped around His waist. The Master carried the basin to the next person—John. As He bent down to wash John's feet, He said patiently, "You do not realize now what I am doing, but later you will understand."

Peter was repelled by the scene. This was their Master, the one they were calling the new King of Israel, and He was on His knees washing their feet as if He were the lowliest servant in the household! There was no way he, Peter, would lower himself to do the job of a common servant.

Peter was next in line, and he knew the Master would come to him next. But Peter wanted none of it. Embarrassment aside, it just wasn't right! No man— least of all a Man with the importance of the Master— should have to wash His followers' feet. That's what servants were for.

The Master dried John's feet and pushed the basin toward Peter. "No," Peter said firmly, looking straight into the Master's eyes. "You will never wash my feet."

The Master shook His head. With tears in His eyes, He said gently, "Unless I wash you, you have no part with Me."

Peter sat pondering the Master's words. Illumination flooded his mind. This wasn't really about washing dirty feet. It was about humility, about taking the lesser path, even when glory was in sight. All the Master's words came back to him. Now he understood what the Master was doing!

"Peter, if I do not wash your feet, you can have no part with Me," the Master repeated.

Peter's reply was barely audible to the others: "Then, Lord, not just my feet but my hands and my head as well!"

The rebellion seeped out of Peter, and he sat quietly as Jesus ministered to him. The other disciples watched in studied silence.

Finally the Master was done. He stood to His feet, rubbing His back. "Do you understand what I have done for you? You call me 'Teacher' and 'Lord,' and rightly so, for that is what I am. Now that I, your Lord and Teacher, have washed your feet, you also should wash one another's feet. I have set you an example that you should do as I have done for you."

When words predominate, actions are slighted. When actions predominate, words bear witness.

The "superstar pastor" era in which we live has done a grave disservice to the New Testament concept of leadership. Coupled with the outrageous excesses of much teaching on submission to authority, many evangelical settings have produced leaders who are untouchable and followers who are passive spectators. The gap of understanding between pulpit and pew has widened to such a degree that leadership is seen as a lofty fantasy, accessible only to those rare individuals having supernatural reserves of charisma and communication skill.

However, merely being able to engagingly transfer information is not good communication, at least not in the Christian leadership context. Communication in this context is about the impartation of ourselves, as reflections of Christ, to those we lead. As such, this type of communication cannot always be linked to the structure of the Sunday morning church service.

The proper—and most effective—setting for teaching others about Christian leadership is found in simple, everyday activities. There, the practical and relevant nature of a relationship with God can be modeled. The servant leader must think, eat, breathe, and sleep modeling, for it is the medium of training future leaders.

In the New Testament context, leadership implies discipleship, and discipleship as modeled by Jesus applies to all areas of life. It is impossible, therefore, for a leader to disciple someone when he is only seen in a hero role. True leadership requires that a leader be seen in pain as well as in victory, in crisis as well as calm, and in sorrow as well as joy.

The servant leader places the utmost priority in being a living demonstration of the relationship between verbal instruction and day-to-day life. Because role-modeling is minimized in the classroom but maximized in everyday life, the servant leader will always be looking for ways to use the situation at hand to exemplify Biblical truth.

Sociological studies have confirmed that all human beings learn most readily by observing role models. In the same way a child needs interactive guidance from his or her parents, our followers need guidance and role-modeling from their leader. A setting where the follower only sees the leader at the front of the church "leading" both distorts and negates the effectiveness of leadership dynamics. Unfortunately, too many leaders are in the habit of using the sermon or lecture format as the primary way in which to instruct those under their charge.

But that is not how it was for the disciples. They were able to observe how Jesus lived and responded to the various situations He faced. They learned first-hand how they should live and conduct themselves.

If we are to extend biblical leadership to others, we can do no less than the Master. We must accept the responsibility to open up our lives to others and model Christlikeness for them.

I recently read Dr. Lawrence Richards' book, *Church Leadership: Following the Example of Jesus Christ.*[15] In it he outlines six principles for effective modeling. As I read them, I marvelled at how completely Jesus modeled the life of faith for His followers, and how much we should be doing the same. When Christ stood after washing the disciples' feet He had truly earned the right to say, "Now that I, your Lord and Teacher, have washed your feet, you also should wash one another's feet. I have set you an example that you should do as I have done for you."

As we examine these six principles, prayerfully evaluate them with respect to how you "model" leadership and the Christian life for your followers.

Frequent, Long-term Contact with the Model

As Jesus began His three years of public ministry, He gathered disciples around Him. Many of these disciples were with Jesus only part time, returning to their fishing or other means of livelihood on occasion. He named twelve of them as His "inner circle," but as we read through the New Testament, we find examples of many other people following Jesus. The twelve, plus others like Joseph of Arimathea, Martha, and Mary enjoyed frequent and long contact with Jesus, the master role-modeler.

A Warm, Loving Relationship with the Model

Jesus often challenged the disciples about their

heart motives, but there is no doubt that He loved those whom He trained, even when they were not lovable! He washed the feet of a doubter, a traitor, and a loud-mouthed, impulsive fisherman. Jesus found a key to their hearts and won their loyalty. After His resurrection, each one served Him until their death.

Exposure to the Inner Elements of the Model

There are no recorded verses in the New Testament where Jesus told someone to go away and mind their own business. That wasn't how Jesus operated, though I am sure He faced the temptation to do so!

Throughout the Gospels, we see that Jesus was approachable and allowed people to see Him for who He was. The gospel writers describe for us times when Jesus was depressed, tired, angry, weary, as well as loving and caring. In short, they saw Him as a normal person responding to the various situations of life that He encountered, and who wasn't ashamed to have people observe His responses.

Observation of the Model in a Variety of Settings

"The Word became flesh and lived for a while among us...full of grace and truth" (John 1:14). I can think of no situation we face today which Jesus did not face with His followers. He mixed freely with prostitutes, Pharisees, Samaritans, rulers, fishermen, farmers, tax collectors, and thieves. Jesus was a model for His followers in everyday situations, and His message was always rooted in and attached to the situation. Money, travel, hospitality, crisis, pain: Jesus used each of these to give living demonstrations of how a leader should respond.

Consistency in the Model's Behavior

Consistency requires that external situations not alter relationships. Jesus was consistent in His obedience to the will of the Father. Jesus always submitted to God's will, even when it meant going to the Cross.

Jesus was consistent to reach out to others in spite of His own pain. On the cross, with thorns digging into His brow and blood dripping from the wounds in His hands and feet, Jesus looked at others. He saw Roman soldiers leering as they ripped His robe apart and cast lots for it. In response, He looked heavenward and prayed, "Father, forgive them, for they do not know what they are doing."

On His left was a thief, a common criminal. Sensing repentance in the man's heart, Jesus offered him reassurance. "I tell you the truth, today you will be with Me in paradise."

Finally, Jesus spotted His mother weeping, and near her, beloved John. Jesus called out, "Dear woman, here is your son," His eyes motioning toward John. And to John He called, "Here is your mother." What compassion, what steadfastness of character He exhibited under extreme duress.

A Correlation Between the Standards of the Model and the Standards of the Group

Jesus did not preach one message to the disciples while secretly living another. Rather, He lived like they did. When He told them to take no money with them, neither did He. When He commanded them to heal the sick, He had already done the same.

There was no instance where Jesus violated His integrity by using one standard for His followers and a lesser standard for Himself. As the ultimate model of integrity, there was a direct correlation between Jesus' personal lifestyle and the lifestyle He encouraged His followers to live.

Of course, we are imperfect beings, and there will be times when our actions are not consistent with our words. That is where humility comes into play.

The most concise definition of humility I have read is that it is "the willingness to be known for who you are." Which is better: to hide behind a facade of spirituality or to allow people to really know us as we are, problems and all?

On the surface, the typical person reasons like this: "I have a lot of personal problems. If people know what I am really like, they will withdraw from me. Therefore, I will not allow people to get too close."

The paradox of humility is that the more people know about us, the more trust they will have in us. The reason is that we develop trust in those who allow us to get to know them, in spite of their obvious weaknesses.

Accountability is another invaluable advantage of leading by example and inviting others to scrutinize our life. Unfortunately, much of the emphasis on accountability today is in the context of organizational structure and flow charts. In addition, many of those highlighting the need for accountability want to apply it downward to those "under" them, while conveniently ignoring any application in their own lives.

But accountability is not purely a function of structure. More properly, it is a function of relationship. A leader cannot sustain a modeling relationship for long if he is a phony! A follower will tolerate flawed reality, but not phony perfectionism. Effective role-modeling presupposes close relationships and therefore serves as a protection to both leader and follower.

If we truly desire to have an impact on others' lives, we must be prepared to spread our life before them. We must be prepared to "dwell among" our followers, exhibiting the same grace and truth to them as Jesus exhibited to His disciples.

Chapter Eight

Inherit the Earth
(Luke 22)

Peter stirred from his sleep. He was vaguely aware something had not been right as he had lain down. Now, in the early hours of the morning, he scoured his mind for what it could be. What was it that had been troubling him? Why was he lying on the ground? Why, why? His fuzzy mind couldn't seem to recall. A voice cut through his searching thoughts. "Are you still sleeping?"

Peter opened his groggy eyes to see the Master staring down at him. Suddenly, everything came rushing back. The Master had asked them to stay and pray with Him, but one by one they had succumbed to fatigue. Guilt flooded Peter.

The Master had been very agitated last night. Peter had never seen Him that way. He had talked almost incoherently about betrayal and death. Peter knew he should have made the effort to stay awake with the Master, but he had been unable to keep his eyes open any longer. It was obvious the Master had not slept. Even in the moonlight Peter could see His shoulders sagging with exhaustion and His bloodshot eyes.

The Master's voice was filled with resignation. "The hour has come. The Son of Man is betrayed into the hands of sinners. Rise! Let us go! Here comes My betrayer!" He gestured to His left.

Peter turned and saw a group of people coming over the brow of the hill, their burning torches marking their progress. Peter hurriedly roused the other disciples from their slumber

As the group approached, Peter hoisted a sword from his belt and took his place beside the Master. He could pick out several people he knew among the crowd. Some of the chief priest's servants, a number of soldiers, and other well-known rabble-rousers from Jerusalem were carrying torches, lanterns, clubs, and other weapons.

Peter winced when he saw the size of the mob. His little band was outnumbered by at least five to one. Was this why the Master had been so melancholy? Was this the end? Was it all over for them?

Judas stepped forward from the midst of the approaching group and walked up to the Master, his eyes darting nervously from side to side. He came close enough for Peter to hear his short, panting breath. "Greetings, Rabbi!" Judas said shakily as he embraced and kissed the Master.

The Master replied, "Friend, do what you came for," and shook His head sadly. Judas evaded the Master's gaze and took a step backward. Aza, the high priest's servant, stepped forward to orchestrate the arrest. Then pandemonium broke out. Men yelled and ran toward the Master, their clubs held high. Two of the largest men, special guards from the temple, attacked Jesus.

Anger flooded Peter's mind. He quickly assessed the situation, looking for a way to escape. Once he freed the Master, they could make a run for it. He tightened his grip on the sword and swung it at one of the guards. The sword crashed sickeningly against the man's skull, sending him to his knees. Blood spurted from the side of the guard's head, and his ear fell into the dust beside him. Glad for the distraction, Peter pulled at the Master. "It's now or never. Let's get out of here."

But the Master did not move. He stood before Aza, blood splattered on the hem of His robe and His eyes fixed on the high priest's servant. Aza felt uneasy, though he was supposed to be in charge. Things felt strangely out of control.

The Master stepped toward the injured guard. The group fell silent, sensing that something was about to happen. The Master picked up the mutilated ear, wiped it on His robe, and reached out to the suffering soldier. The Master gently placed the man's ear in the correct position and pressed it with His palm. The bleeding immediately stopped.

The Master held His hand over the ear a few seconds, and when He drew His hand back, the whole group gasped. The guard's ear was completely normal—healed. There were no marks, no scars, nothing to indicate that only moments ago it had been sliced off with a sword.

Aza coughed nervously. He had a job to do, and a little trickery was not going to deter him. But neither of the guards heeded him when he motioned for them to arrest the Master.

"Put your sword back in its place," said the Master, turning to Peter. Then, looking directly at Aza, He said: "For all who draw the sword will die by the sword. Don't you think that I could appeal to My Father, and He would send more than twelve legions of angels to rescue Me? But then how would Scripture be fulfilled?"

Aza fumed. "Seize Him," he barked to the guards. The guards shook their heads and stepped back into the crowd. They no longer had the stomach for this.

Other guards stepped forward to take their place and
the Master was led away. Peter and the other disciples
followed behind, baffled by the night's events.

---

*The leader who walks in meekness is forever liberated
from the burden of needing to get back at people who have
hurt him or have taken advantage of him.*

If you had been in the garden that night, how
would you have interpreted Jesus' actions? If Jesus
had enough power to reattach a soldier's ear, then He
surely had enough power to save Himself from the
situation. But why didn't He use it? He had the re-
sources to alter the outcome of the situation, but made
a deliberate choice not to use them. Many would view
this as weakness. The Bible describes it as meekness.

"Have you ever noticed the number of times Jesus
refused to use power?" asks Richard Foster. A few
paragraphs later he goes on to say: "The power that
comes from above is not filled with bravado and bom-
bast. It lacks the symbols of human authority; indeed,
its symbols are a manger and a cross. It is power that
is not recognized as power. It is a self-chosen position
of meekness that to human eyes looks powerless. The
power from above leads from weakness."[16]

I remember vividly my first encounter with meekness. I was eight years old and lived in a neighborhood bursting with boys around my own age. All of
us were sports fanatics who spent every spare moment honing our imagined athletic skills on the basketball court at the back of the high school. "Eric" was
my hero during those days. He was several years
older than me and his prowess on the court was un-
matched.

One sunny Saturday we all gathered at the court
for a game of basketball. Eric was there, and we were

joined by a nineteen year old who had recently married Eric's sister. Because Eric and his brother-in-law were the tallest, they were on opposite sides, guarding each other. The game was close and competitive. In fact, it began to get quite rough.

Eric and his brother-in-law were battling for a rebound when suddenly the brother-in-law exploded in anger. He turned on Eric and began pummeling his face.

I came from a quiet and disciplined home, and seeing one family member beating on another came as a shock to me. Even more surprising was Eric's response. He put his hands down at his sides and passively allowed the punches and slaps to bloody his face.

Finally, I couldn't stand it a moment longer. I yelled, "Come on, Eric. Fight back. You're tougher than he is. What's the matter? Are you a chicken?"

Eric stoically stood his ground until his brother-in-law jumped into his car and raced off. The gang of little eight-year-olds silently disappeared, stunned at the swiftness of Eric's defeat.

I followed Eric inside his house. He walked calmly over to the sink, turned on the faucet, and wincing, began washing the blood from his face.

"Why didn't you fight back?" I asked, completely baffled by Eric's behavior.

Eric turned to look at me through swollen, purple eyes. "I'll tell you why," he said. "A couple of months ago, we got into a fight over something he said about my sister. I did pretty well. But when it was over, he told me that if I ever stood up to him again, he would go home and beat up my sister. I know he means it. I don't care what happens; I'm not going to let him hurt my sister, even if it means getting beat up myself."

My naive mind reeled with newfound insight. Eric

was really a hero. His apparent weakness in receiving the beating was not the true picture. I saw that facts do not always adequately explain the truth. The *fact* was that Eric did get beaten up. The *truth* was that Eric could have retaliated, but he had enough strength of character to restrain himself in order to protect someone he loved.

Eric was meek, but not weak. A lesser person may have buckled during the beating and begun swinging his fists, but not Eric. Compassion for his sister constrained him.

The same was true of Jesus at His arrest. Legions of angels could have come to His rescue had He just said the word. I imagine the disciples could have put up a good fight in their own right. But compassion constrained Jesus. Something higher was at stake, so Jesus willingly submitted to His arrest.

Servant leaders must take their lead from the Master's example at His arrest. We must become people of meekness. And as Christ reminded us in the Beatitudes, "The meek shall inherit the earth." Why? Because the meek will be the only people with enough strength of character to rule and reign with Christ without their egos getting in the way.

But what does it mean to lead from the place of meekness? It obviously doesn't imply that a leader should be a spineless individual with weak resolve. Nor does it mean that he should be indecisive and hesitant, or always mouthing pious platitudes about the virtues of nothingness.

Scottish preacher James S. Stewart sums it up this way: "It is always upon human weakness and humiliation, not human strength and confidence, that God chooses to build his kingdom; and that he can use us not merely in spite of our ordinariness and helplessness and disqualifying infirmities, but precisely because of them."[17]

Because of this, true biblical leadership often goes unnoticed or misinterpreted. The reason is simple: fallen man is a hero worshiper, and as such is drawn to heroic, larger-than-life images. Knowing this, Satan attempted to lure Jesus away from the path of the Cross and onto the platform of fanfare. The tantalizing temptations served up by the Enemy were all centered in spectacular feats designed to induce hero worship.

Had Jesus succumbed to the allure of showy displays of strength, the world would have indeed followed Him—right to the pinnacle of megalomania! It is no wonder then, that those in attendance at the Crucifixion were an unsympathetic mob, most anxious to heap cruel invective upon Jesus. From their limited perspective, Jesus was weak—an object of scorn rather than honor.

In Scripture, humility has primarily to do with the vertical relationship of man to God. As stated in I Peter 5:6, "Humble yourselves, therefore, under God's mighty hand." Leadership and all other acts of service in God's Kingdom are measured by humility.

Meekness is the opposite side of the coin. It is a fruit of God's grace which is exhibited primarily in the horizontal relationship of man to man. Charles Finney said:

> Meekness, a phenomenon of the will, and as an attribute of benevolence, is the opposite both of resistance to injury and retaliation. It is properly and strictly forbearance under injurious treatment.[18]

Our mistreatment always comes from other human beings. At times, someone may attempt to take advantage of us by sharing our weaknesses with others. The meek person does not fear the truth, even about himself. While he may feel a sense of betrayal at being exposed by someone he allowed to view him in a vulnerable state, his meekness does not allow him to retaliate.

"But," some may ask, "if a leader allows his followers to see him in a vulnerable state, won't the followers use that against the leader at a later time?" The answer is simple—"Yes, the risk is great!" The fine line between humility and humiliation resides in the choice one makes to be either open or closed in regard to personal struggles.

Jesus knew the risk and made Himself vulnerable anyway. Despite knowing that within twenty-four hours Peter, James, and John would all deny knowing Him, He still allowed them to see His anguish.

Beyond this truth, however, resides an equally important reality: God has deliberately chosen the weak to achieve His purposes. According to the apostle Paul in I Corinthians 1:26-29:

> Brothers, think of what you were when you were called. Not many of you were wise by human standards; not many were influential; not many were of noble birth. But God chose the foolish things of the world to shame the wise; God chose the weak things of the world to shame the strong. He chose the lowly things of this world and the despised things—and the things that are not—to nullify the things that are, so that no one may boast before him.

J. Oswald Sanders reinforces this truth by stating that, "Although Paul himself was an intellectual, he gloried in the fact that God had purposefully not chosen the intellectual, highborn, powerful, and influential. Instead he chose people who were weak in ability, influence, or even in body—those disregarded by the world—to achieve his purposes of blessing."[19]

To the servant leader, leading from meekness means that the leader is totally honest with himself and others about his own weakness, seeking neither to cover it up or flaunt it in a self-pitying way. He moves ahead in loving obedience to God in spite of his frailty, therefore of necessity, abandoning himself to God's power and grace. Lasting fruit is never harvested by self-reliant planters, but only by those who understand that God's "power is made perfect in weakness" (II Corinthians 12:9).

Dwight L. Moody, the Billy Graham of his day, learned to exploit the power of weakness as Paul did. He was innocent of education, his physical appearance was unattractive, and his voice was high-pitched and nasal. But his conscious weakness did not prevent God from shaking the world through him.

On one occasion, a press reporter was assigned to cover his campaigns in order to discover the secret of his extraordinary power and influence over people of all social strata. After he returned from his assignment, he wrote, "I can see nothing whatever in Moody to account for his marvelous work."

When Moody was told this, he chuckled, "Of course not, because the work was God's, not mine." Moody's weakness was God's weapon.[20]

Servant leadership does not require that we cease using our natural, God-given gifts. It does require that we cease our reliance upon them. Instead, we must learn to cast our reliance unceasingly upon the God who loves to lead His children.

Chapter Nine

A Second Chance
(Luke 24)

The three men sat huddled together in the corner on the floor. Golden slivers of sunlight burst through the cracks in the shutters, casting pools of light onto the dusty floor. It was dawn, but they had been awake for hours, just sitting and staring into the darkness.

"Who would have thought it?" Bartholomew said, voicing his thoughts aloud. "A week ago we were part of the huge welcome—the palm leaves, the cheering, and the accolades."

"Do not be afraid, O Daughter of Zion; see, your king is coming, seated on a donkey's colt," intoned Philip, more for his own hearing than anyone else's.

Bartholomew slammed the side of his fist against the floor. "Why didn't we see it? We could have stopped Judas if we'd known."

Philip shrugged his shoulders. "There was no way of knowing. Judas must have been planning it for a long while. Did you see the way the guards greeted him? They acted like old friends."

"Joseph told me the chief priest gave Judas thirty pieces of silver for his effort." Tears brimmed in Bartholomew's eyes as he spoke.

"Well, Judas got what he deserved. I hear they found him hanging from a tree. Killed himself," offered Philip, hoping the news would in some way atone for the treachery of their former comrade.

"We should all be dead," interjected Peter, speaking for the first time. "I was just as bad. When the Master asked me to pray with Him in the garden, I fell asleep. We all did. If we had stayed awake, things might have been different. We couldn't even stay awake when He wanted us to."

Peter paused to collect his thoughts. "And then when I was sitting in the courtyard and the servant girl asked me if I was with Him, I said, 'no.' What was the point of aligning myself with a doomed Man? I did it three times.

"But do you know what the worst part was? Jesus knew. He *knew*. He knew I would do that." Peter glanced at his two colleagues: dark, shadowy lumps in the gloomy room. "The night He washed our feet, He knew. He told me then that I would betray Him three times. And He knew what Judas was up to. It was as if He wanted it to happen. I don't understand how, but He knew. He knew we'd each betray Him in our own way."

The room fell silent. Their ease with each other now played against them. Each knew what the others were thinking, and what they had done. There was no hiding behind a curtain of lies, no need for pretense.

What was there to live for now? They had all left their livelihoods to follow the Master. They had believed He was the Messiah, and that they were part of a vast new order He would bring to change the world. Now it was over, and they were all partly to blame.

"I wish I could go back. I should have stayed with Him at the Cross," said Bartholomew after a few minutes. "I didn't even have the courage to do that. His mother stayed with Him, but I didn't...."

"We are marked men, whether we were with Him

at the end or not," interjected Peter. "Yesterday the guards came to my uncle's house asking for me. He told them he hadn't seen me for days, but they searched anyway, turning the place upside down."

"Do you think it's safer for us to stick together or to go our separate ways?" asked Philip. Somehow they needed to pull their thoughts together. The three men were in great danger.

The city swarmed with soldiers and indignant Jewish leaders. Priests and Roman soldiers had made an absurd but deadly alliance. And now that they had blood on their hands, they were likely to want the problem dealt with completely. They wouldn't want the "Christ problem" to raise its head again, and the remaining disciples were part of the Christ problem.

"I don't know about the Master. I don't think anything we could have done would have saved Him," said Bartholomew, ignoring Philip's question.

"I watched Him. It was as if He wanted to die in the end. When Pilate was asking Him questions, He wouldn't answer. Pilate pressed Him hard. I think he wanted to let the Master go, but the Master would say nothing."

They slumped into silence once more. Their emotions swirled from grief over the betrayal of their Master to contempt and anger for the one who had betrayed Him. But more than anything they felt an intolerable burden—they had each betrayed the Master. Cowardice, unreliability, feebleness, and fear were no longer abstract concepts reserved for others who were weaker.

The pain each was experiencing denied them the luxury of pointing the finger at anyone else. When the harsh, illuminating beam of adversity had glared upon them, all their character flaws had been mercilessly exposed.

They talked for hours, lapsing in and out of grief, anger, frustration, and disappointment. Finally, they agreed that it would be less dangerous for them if the disciples stayed together as a group. Alone, they could be picked off. As a group, they could defend each other.

It took more than a day before word reached all the scattered disciples. Chaos reigned in Jerusalem. The rumor mill was spinning. There were all kinds of conflicting reports. Some said that Jesus' body had been stolen by the disciples; others said that He had risen and that His grave clothes were still wadded up in the tomb.

Whatever the explanation, one thing became clear on the third day: the tomb where they had buried the Master was now empty. Peter went to the tomb to see for himself. There was no explanation. Peter walked away, scratching his head and pondering.

Finally the disciples made their way to the prearranged meeting place. When the last of them had arrived, James heaved the door shut and dropped a heavy wooden bar into place. If anyone wanted to enter now, they would have to contend with a four-inch-thick oak door.

James turned and surveyed his comrades. It was the first time they had been together since the night of betrayal. How different they all looked now.

Then James' eye caught Peter's expression. He seemed animated, even cheerful. James raised his eyebrows; there was no telling what grief and guilt could do to a person.

Peter cleared his throat as he stood to address the group. A broad smile wreathed his face as he began. "Like you, at first my heart was torn inside me. But now I understand." The disciples listened, unsure of the direction Peter was taking them. "Yesterday I was on my way to Emmaus with another man who had once been a follower of the Master. I was confused by all that had happened and wanted to leave it behind."

Philip and Bartholomew looked at each other, surprised. Peter was the one who had finally insisted that they all stay together in Jerusalem.

"As we walked along, we were joined by a Man who didn't seem to know anything about what had gone on with the Master. So we began filling Him in." As Peter became more excited, his gestures emphasized the importance of his words.

"Finally we came to an inn and stopped for dinner. As we sat with the Stranger to eat, He took bread, gave thanks for it, and offered us each a piece. At that moment it was as though a cloud was lifted from our eyes. It was Him! The Stranger was the Master, but before we could say anything, He disappeared."

"Are you sure?" asked Andrew.

"I won't believe it until I see Him with my own eyes," grumbled Thomas. "And why didn't you recognize Him straight away?"

"Let him talk. I want to hear," interjected James. "This fits with the things Mary Magdalene said."

Before Peter could say anything more, another voice sounded in the room: "Peace be with you!"

They shrank back in instantaneous recognition, eyes wide, mouths agape. It was the Master!

He held His hands out to them. Each disciple recognized those hands. They were hands which had reached out lovingly and tenderly to them many times. Now a jagged scar marred their symmetry. No, not marred—adorned.

A collective gasp escaped from the lips of the stunned disciples, followed immediately by the dawning of joyous revelation. Their eyes were still wide, but no longer fearful. An intoxicating wave of joy rolled over them.

Peter watched as the Master surveyed the room, His eyes resting fondly on each disciple. When His gaze reached Peter, the Master stopped and looked long and penetratingly at him. Peter could feel the tears welling in his eyes. He looked back at the Master, a question forming in his mind. *Me, Lord? After all I have done? Me? You want to trust me again?*

There was no need for Peter to voice the question; the Master had read it in his eyes. He nodded gently, and Peter felt the glow of God's trust and acceptance wash over him. A flood of tears cascaded down his cheeks and the burly fisherman unashamedly fell at the feet of his Master.

Trust conferred is an act of emancipation. Trust betrayed is an act of violence.

Jesus placed the responsibility for establishing His Church in the unsure hands of eleven abject failures. David Watson aptly describes the situation:

> The disciples of Jesus were very ordinary people, with all the human faults and failings that we often see in ourselves. Because of the integrity of the Gospels, we see the disciples as ambitious, selfish, argumentative, weak in faith, anxious, fearful, impulsive, immature in words and actions, proud in the face of temptation, lethargic in prayer, impatient with the children, weary of crowds, bewildered and depressed by the events leading to the crucifixion. We notice how slow they were to learn, how quickly they forgot even the most dramatic spiritual lessons. In other words, they were just like most of us! Yet these were the men that Jesus chose to be disciples and

trained to be leaders.[21]

It is truly remarkable that God chose to use the eleven disciples to change the world forever. It is even more astonishing that He chooses to use us! In Paul's letter to the Corinthians, he voices the wonder of God using sinful men. "For God, who said, 'Let light shine out of darkness,' made his light shine in our hearts to give us the light of the knowledge of the glory of God in the face of Christ. But we have this treasure in jars of clay to show that this all-surpassing power is from God and not from us" (II Corinthians 4:6-7).

Jesus' leadership example, as shown through the way He entrusted His perfect message to imperfect men, may be the hardest principle of all for us to emulate. Jesus modeled, trained, and commissioned. Then He left! The apostle Paul later copied this technique. In fact, most of Paul's leadership was exercised from jail cells! What a contrast to the methods we employ today.

Although we are all imperfect, our tendency is to demand perfection from others before trusting and releasing them into leadership. It will be a long wait! Our current practice seems to be to train, and train, and train. Then we hold on by trying to persuade our trainees that they owe allegiance to us because we trained them. In other words, we want those we train to be attached to our ministry—at least until they begin to be a problem to us.

What is the fruit of our leadership in terms of releasing others? Are there many who have been trained and released into their own ministries, or to function with us or even over us? Do we take joy in seeing our followers embark upon their own ministries, even if they never relate to us as a leader again? Are we thrilled or threatened when they eclipse our leadership in terms of scope and influence?

He who was the ultimate Leader not only trained, He trusted. Furthermore, it gave Him joy to announce that His pupils would do greater things than their Leader.

A common criticism arising during discussions about releasing people (especially young people) into leadership roles is that they don't hàve enough experience to lead. One must ask how they acquire experience if they aren't allowed to exercise leadership!

Could it be that some leaders are afraid to give others, especially youth, a chance to lead for fear that they might err, and in erring, be an embarrassment to the one who allowed them to try? Isn't such a fear rooted in a self-centered desire to protect one's reputation rather than in a true desire to guard against releasing a leader too prematurely?

The servant leader will always resist the inclination to load increasingly stringent qualifications on potential leaders. He wants to free them, not bind them with weights too heavy to bear. He understands that a major part of leadership is to provide an atmosphere of trust and freedom. Only in this environment can leadership develop to its full potential.

Too often, leaders do the opposite. They erect an extensive framework of qualifications, ostensibly to better prepare the prospective young leader for his job. The sad irony is that if the older leader would have faced those same requirements when he was young, he probably could not have fulfilled them.

Trust is the most fragile component in the mix of ingredients that make up healthy relationships.[22] The servant leader understands that honor and trust always go together. Therefore, he seeks to honor his followers by both investing trust in them and demonstrating his own trustworthiness. This trust is best demonstrated by training a follower and then releasing him into increasing levels of leadership.

The carnal leader will insist that his followers trust him, often berating those who dare to question his authority. This thinking circumvents the truth that followers, in the long run, will not follow a leader they do not trust. Furthermore, trust demanded from others, but not extended to others, always leaves the follower with a sense of violation.

This brings us to an important principle. The initial responsibility to demonstrate trust must first rest with the individual possessing the greatest authority.[23] A leader honors his followers when he proves his own trustworthiness to them. However, when a leader betrays trust, his followers are shamed and dishonored.

God willingly entrusted His only Son into the hands of mortal parents. Jesus willingly entrusted the message of the Gospel to feeble men. There are times when as a servant leader, humility will require that you submit and entrust yourself to leaders who might be of lesser position, have less experience, or who could have a weaker character than you. Such action builds the other person up while also serving as a reminder that we are all people under authority.

Such a scenario was played out during my first outreach with Youth With A Mission. Though I was immature, I had been assigned as leader of a team of fifteen young people who would spend two weeks witnessing in Paris, France. The only housing available for the two weeks was in an old, dilapidated theater that was being used as a church. The facilities were woefully inadequate, having only one bathroom, and it contained only a sink and a toilet.

Three days into the outreach, Loren Cunningham (founder of Youth With A Mission) arrived to visit. I was excited to see him, and even more excited to learn

that he was planning to spend a few days with us. I
didn't know Loren very well. I expected him to stay
at a nearby hotel. It came as quite a shock when he
asked me, "Denny, where do you want me to sleep?"

"What do you mean, where do I want you to
sleep?" I stammered, embarrassed to have to explain
our inadequate facilities. "You're the boss. Don't you
sleep wherever you want?"

I will never forget the patient, gentle look on
Loren's face as he replied, "No, Denny, you're the
leader of this team. While I am here, I am under your
leadership. Where do you want me to sleep?"

I was stunned, but there was no place of "honor"
which I could allocate to Loren as his quarters. "Follow me," I finally instructed him, as I headed up some
dingy stairs. The girls on the team had placed their
sleeping bags up in the balcony and walled the area
off with sheets.

We single men had set up our quarters on the stage
at the front of the theater, and had attempted to wall
it off. The area was rather small and each of us had
defined our personal "space" by surrounding our
sleeping bags with chairs and suitcases.

I was about to offer my carefully defended spot to
Loren when I noticed him eyeing the grand piano.
Surely he didn't want us to move it! There was no-
where for it to go. Instead, Loren bent down and
examined the space available under the piano. Without thinking, I blurted out, "You can sleep under the
piano, if you like." Loren nodded, smiled graciously,
and said, "That sounds just fine to me."

Even though that incident took place twenty-three
years ago, its impact was so great upon me that I still
remember every detail. I was deeply impressed and
humbled at the same time. Here was the founder of a
successful ministry, graciously submitting to my im-

mature leadership.

Not only did Loren die to the right of personal comfort, he also encouraged my development as a fledgling leader by purposely putting himself in the place of depending upon me for direction. His example did more to shape my perspective on biblical leadership than any book I could have read or sermon I could have heard. My only hope is that I have been able to take his example and live it out before others.

We must never be afraid of placing ourselves in positions of need or dependency. It is proper to want to minister to others, as long as we realize that part of ministering to others is allowing them to minister to us. Doing this, especially with a younger leader, speaks a loud message that we trust him. In so doing, our gracious response may be a catalyst to release a hidden gift of leadership in a follower.

That which allows a leader to release people into their own ministry can be summed up in one simple word—faith. All leaders display faith in one form or another. Some place their faith in the quality of a training program. For others, it is faith in their own leadership ability. In both instances, the shallowness of faith will be exposed by the inability of the leader to trust those whom he releases. Faith always requires the extension of trust, but that trust must be in God, not in our ability, the trainees' ability, or the strength of our program.

The ability to extend trust to frail mortals displays the depth and quality of faith one has in God. Jesus, having great faith in His Father and demonstrating that faith by His obedience to the Father's will, placed more trust in the disciples than they would have placed in themselves.

The awe-inspiring greatness of Christ's splendor is not defined by the power of His natural attributes,

but by the unfathomable depth of character He exhibited in entrusting the developing and equipping of
His Church into the hands of mortal leaders. And He
does the same today!

Conclusion

This book begins a journey for each of us who leads. It is an intensely personal pilgrimage which inspires us to examine each aspect of our leadership. We must travel the road out of public view. The events taking place in the sanctuary of our heart determine the quality of true Godly servanthood. Clearly, the essence of true servanthood is "hidden-ness."

Jesus-style leadership requires a humble commitment to serve others, regardless of the cost or the rewards. Christian leadership is the ultimate form of stewardship. It is a daunting task to take on the responsibility for training and bringing to a place of personal wholeness and freedom those we lead.

Thus, our reason for being leaders must reside in the nature and being of God Himself. "Your attitude should be the same as that of Christ Jesus: Who, being in very nature God, did not consider equality with God something to be grasped, but made himself nothing, taking the very nature of a servant, being made in human likeness" (Philippians 2:5-7). Any notion of leadership divorced from Christ's model of making Himself nothing can only be labeled as carnal.

It is time for nothing less than a revolutionary new leadership thrust to take place. The key aspect of this revolution must be that there is only one standard by which to define true leadership, and that is Jesus Himself. Learn from other leaders. Admire and respect them. But pattern yourself after only One.

May each of us be found following Jesus...through the dust.

A student is not above his teacher, nor a servant above his master. It is enough for the student to be like his teacher, and the servant like his master...."

Matthew 10:24-25

Notes

1—M. Scott Peck, *The Different Drum* (New York: Simon and Schuster, 1987), p. 99.

2—Henri J.M. Nouwen, *The Wounded Healer* (Image Books, 1979), p. 71.

3—Francois de Fenelon, *Fenelon's Spiritual Letters* (Christian Books Publishing House, 1982), p. 229.

4—Nouwen, *The Wounded Healer*, p. 71.

5—Henri J. M. Nouwen, *In the Name of Jesus* (The Crossroad Publishing Co., 1989), p. 62. This short treatise on leadership is startling in its simplicity, but deeply profound in its impact.

6—Richard J. Foster, *Money, Sex, and Power* (San Francisco: Harper and Row Publishers, 1985), p. 219.

7—Fenelon, *Fenelon's Spiritual Letters*, p. 204.

8—Foster, *Money, Sex, and Power*, p. 243.

9—Gayle D. Erwin, *The Jesus Style* (Word Books, 1983), p. 73.

10—Nouwen, *In the Name of Jesus*, p. 60.

11—Erwin, *The Jesus Style*, p. 55.

12—The words *submit* and *subject*—found in I Corinthians 16:16, Ephesians 5:22, James 4:7, and I Peter 5:5—all mean "a voluntary yielding in love." It is neither a legislative nor a military term.

13—Foster, *Money, Sex, and Power*, p. 26.

14—J. Oswald Sanders, *Paul the Leader* (NavPress, 1984), p. 140.

15—Dr. Lawrence Richards, *Church Leadership: Following the Example of Jesus Christ* (Zondervan, 1988).

16—Foster, *Money, Sex, and Power*, p. 203-204.

17—Sanders, *Paul the Leader*, p. 173-174.

18—Charles G. Finney, *Lectures on Systematic Theology* (Colporter Kemp, 1944), p. 169.

19—Sanders, *Paul the Leader*, p. 175.

20—Sanders, *Paul the Leader*, p. 176.

21—David Watson, *Called and Committed: World-Changing Discipleship* (Wheaton: Harold Shaw Publishers, 1982), p. 49.

22—From lectures given by Tom Marshall in Amsterdam, May 1987.

23—From lectures given by Tom Marshall in Amsterdam, May 1987.